WINNING NUMBERS

How to Use Business Facts and Figures to Make Your Point and Get Ahead

Michael C. Thomsett

American Management Association

This publication is designed to provide accurate and authoritative information in regard to the subject matter covered. It is sold with the understanding that the publisher is not engaged in rendering legal, accounting, or other professional service. If legal advice or other expert assistance is required, the services of a competent professional person should be sought.

Library of Congress Cataloging-in-Publication Data

Thomsett, Michael C.
    Winning numbers : how to use business facts and figures to make your point and get ahead / Michael C. Thomsett.
    p. cm.
  ISBN 0-8144-5958-7
  1. Business presentations. 2. Managerial accounting. I. Title.
HF5718.22.T47   1990   89-81029
658.15—dc20   CIP

Printing number

10 9 8 7 6 5 4

Contents

Introduction

The Role of the Numbers

You are preparing for a meeting this afternoon. On the agenda are several topics that will affect your department, including whether to increase your payroll budget. You know you need to hire more people, but you're not so certain that you can present your arguments in such a way that you can win approval. Your task: to present a series of facts clearly enough that management will agree with your point of view.

Decision makers must be constantly aware of the bottom line. So the question of cost and profit always exists, spoken or unspoken. You can make your requests in one of two ways: by presenting a problem and asking for a solution, or by proposing an idea that solves your problem and the problem the decision maker faces.

Accounting is the pivotal science by which organizations judge their own performance. The measurement of profit and growth depends on what the numbers reveal. So when you approach a problem with profits in mind, you increase your own value to management.

As a nonaccounting manager, you will be able to upgrade your degree of participation in organizational growth by mastering the science of numbers. This is not to suggest that a nonaccounting manager should change emphasis or that the numbers are the only revealing factors in company life. To the contrary, the numbers are only a small area of management concern. The accountant, however, often holds a distinct advantage over the nonaccountant in several respects.

- *Communication.* Accountants are used to communicating in terms of profit and loss. Numbers are the language of business, and every nonaccounting manager will benefit by learning to think in those terms.
- *Influence.* Profit and loss reporting holds great importance in the company so that the accountant often has a natural advantage over other managers. Once you learn to communicate in terms of profit, investment, and financial risk, your internal influence will grow.
- *Planning.* Preparing for the future is a nonfinancial process. Yet the creation of growth capital, control over costs and expenses, and allocation of resources depend on your ability to explain objectives— whether profits are involved or not—in financial terms.

Example: You want to expand the floor space in your department. You can present your argument for this idea in two ways. First, you can state, "We need more space." Or, you might argue, "Providing more floor space will save the company money."

If the second argument is backed up with facts, it will be difficult to dispute your argument. In comparison, the plea for more space is relatively ineffective. Remember that management considers every request in financial terms.

This example demonstrates how a solution-based form of communication increases your effectiveness. You will be perceived as a decisive, valuable member of the team once you begin communicating in financial terms. Accountants already understand this idea because they deal with numbers on a daily basis and normally communicate in financial terms.

This book helps you to master the financial skills needed to communicate, gain influence, and plan for your department and your career. Not emphasized are the techniques for setting up books, or for reporting on profits; that is the task of the accounting department. What is shown is how to make the best use of financial information as it applies in your nonaccounting environment.

By working with the accounting department, you can develop an alliance rather than an adversarial relationship. Once you begin applying the financial point of view in communication, influence, and planning, your accounting department will respect your approach, and that, too, will help to make the interdepartmental relationship a positive one.

This book also explains the major functions performed by the accounting department, not to show you how to become an accountant but to demonstrate how these skills can and should be used by all managers. These functions are to record information; to interpret the numbers and to give them meaning; and to report that meaning. A fourth function is to anticipate the future, managed through the budgeting process. And the fifth is to control, to recognize emerging trends and actions required to monitor and change the future.

Every result or outcome—even those far removed from the numbers themselves—can be measured in financial terms. When you become a communicator of financial information, top management will judge you not just on the profitability of your department but also on your ability to communicate in terms they understand—in *their* language.

Chapter 1

A Method for Keeping Score

Success or failure, profit or loss, growth or stagnation. Judgments about how well a business is being run and whether it is meeting its objectives are decided on the basis of financial information. The problem, though, is that although most judgments made by management are concerned with numbers, the outcome of those judgments affect people.

As a nonaccounting manager, you deal with human issues, but your environment is profit-oriented. If your company's management makes decisions based solely on financial information, then the accountants in your organization may have greater influence than other managers. This advantage may affect every point of communication and planning. Top management may look to the numbers for answers, even when the issues are strictly human ones.

Accountants are expected to play a significant and responsible role, and top management may assume much concerning the proper role of the accounting department. Just as you are at a disadvantage because you are not accustomed to purely financial issues, Accounting often is cast in the role of adviser to top management, even on issues that should be determined at the top.

THE PURPOSE OF KEEPING RECORDS

The nonaccounting manager probably sees the accounting department as the place where records are kept, where financial statements are drawn up, and where budgets are prepared. While all of this describes some accounting functions, the picture is incomplete.

The accounting department documents the results of what goes on in the company. Records exist for a number of important reasons. First is the legal requirement to document income, costs, and expenses for tax purposes. In this role, the accountant is a collector of facts.

But financial information is used for much more than just the collecting of facts. Accountants are responsible for developing and operating routines to interpret information and anticipate the future; for reporting to management on the significance of emerging trends; for budgeting for future profits, capital expenditures, and cash flow; and for controlling the use of available funds.

Without these functions, few businesses would be able to keep their doors open. The methodical and thorough control of finances is essential to every operation. Ask almost anyone who has failed in business, and they will tell you immediately. More than any other factor, the lack of financial control prevents success, whether the company is a one-owner shop or a multibillion-dollar corporation.

Accounting's scorekeeping functions affect you as a non-accounting manager. First, you are directly affected by the actions, recommendations, and conclusions the accountant reaches and by the decisions made by top management in response. Second, the critical nature of financial information places the accounting department in a position of great power and influence in the company. In some respects, this degree of influence is appropriate; but when the emphasis is excessive, management's perspectives are not as healthy as they would be by looking at the broader picture, which should involve gathering information from all sources.

In some companies, management is more likely to listen to the accountant's advice than to advice offered from others. In other companies, management distrusts the accountants and views them as lacking in creativity and vision. Both extreme points of view are unfair. Accountants rarely have all of the answers, but they invariably make valuable contributions. A soundly managed company is one in which everyone is given the chance to contribute.

Recognizing that accountants employ a number of very useful analytical techniques, you will discover the tremendous potential waiting for you in financially oriented communication. If you apply that potential in your own internal functions, then the power of financial reporting will be within your grasp.

INFORMATION ANALYSIS

The difference between accountants and other department managers often is found in the approach to problems. The best way to communicate with top management is to offer solutions to problems, rather than to expect someone else to solve a problem for you.

Your first change in focus should be to develop a keen awareness of solutions. Don't ever bring a problem to your supervisor without having one or more recommended solutions ready. If you assume the responsibility for arriving at a solution, you will be seen as a valuable resource, as someone who can be depended on for answers, not just as another of the multitude that constantly bombards the boss with questions, requests, and demands.

Accept the fact that top management must consider the profit and loss aspects of every question. That's part of its job. So you strengthen your arguments whenever you are able to express solutions and requests—even of the most human nature—in terms of reduced expenses, increased profits, and improved productivity.

Example: The marketing director in a software manufacturing company has concluded that newspaper ads are less effective than direct mail. The accounting department recently completed a preliminary budget, which included plans for increasing newspaper ad expenses.

The marketing manager attends a budget review meeting. When the subject of advertising comes up, he states, "Direct mail is more

effective than newspaper ads." The accountant responds that newspaper ads reach more people for less money spent and that it is a more
efficient way to spend advertising dollars. The accountant supports
the claim with circulation figures.

The simple presentation of fact is a difficult argument to
fight. Unfortunately, "fact" in this case is not related to the
real issue—that placing newspaper ads means less response,
less volume, and less profit. The marketing manager has no
facts of his own to prove this point. So he comes back with
the only argument he has: "I don't like newspaper advertisement."

That argument is useless and, in all likelihood, makes
the marketing manager appear unprofessional, possibly
harming his reputation. The issue was not whether one side
or the other was right or wrong. The accountant did a little
research and drew a conclusion from the discovered facts.

There is nothing devious in presenting this assumption.
The marketing manager, unused to dealing with the numbers, is at a disadvantage. The accountant lacks the insight
about effective advertisement, so he makes a recommendation based on the facts he does have.

The marketing manager could have avoided the frustration of losing an argument if he had gathered a few facts of
his own. With a focus on profits, his arguments would be
strong ones. He could report that newspaper advertising
does not produce an acceptable return on the investment,
whereas direct mail does. And he would be prepared to
prove that point with facts and recent financial information.

The argument that he did "not like" newspaper ads was
emotional. His meaning might have been expressed as, "I
don't like them because they don't work," but that's not what
was expressed. A nonaccounting manager might depend on
intuition and experience to a large degree, when accountants will invariably depend on facts and proof. Your intuition may be a valuable attribute because it's based on
experience and common sense. But remember, intuition is
not proof, and a financially based argument is often the
strongest and most compelling reason behind management's

final decision. You need your intuition to contribute, but like the accountant, you can use a financial focus to strengthen your argument.

A VALUABLE MANAGEMENT TOOL

Intuition can serve as a strong and necessary weapon in your management arsenal. Unfortunately, though, you must park your intuition in the hallway when you enter a meeting. Inside that room, you will be respected more for the facts and ideas you contribute than for what you sense.

You can have it both ways: You can depend on intuition to lead your department, and you can support your decisions and positions with well-researched facts. You can take a stand supported with facts and still apply the intangible qualities that create good leaders and managers.

When you consider the advantage that accountants often have over other managers, you will realize why their level of influence is greater. This influence is demonstrated in the fact that accountants have a better chance of being promoted to top executive spots than any other manager. A survey conducted by *Forbes* reported that 30 percent of the chief executive officers in 850 of the largest corporations in the United States were people with accounting and financial backgrounds—more than from any other field. The Institute of Management Accountants commented on this survey: "A future in management accounting holds the promise of advancement, with accompanying rewards, even to the topmost positions in the largest corporations."

Accountants advance more rapidly to top positions not because they are accountants but because of the way they communicate, influence, and plan. The skill required to master these attributes is not unique to the accounting profession, but the practice is more common among accountants. The numbers are their lives.

The discipline is not just learned in school. It's a focus that happens to fit with management's style. So if you approach every issue with scorekeeping in mind, you too will be in a position to advance in the company. The classic adversarial relationship between the two broad camps in a company is well known. On one side are the number-crunchers, accountants, and administrators. On the other are the marketing people.

From Marketing's point of view, accountants are nothing more than clerks, preoccupied with the bottom line. They do not care about the customer and have probably never even met one. They understand only budgets, profits, and rules. To make things worse, the perception is that the accountant fails to understand that to make money, you must spend money.

From Accounting's point of view, marketing people have no respect for the need to plan and manage. They think only of sales, commissions, and volume. They don't take the time to fill out a report correctly, and they have no respect for the budget.

Somewhere in between these stereotypical extremes is the successful and respected manager/diplomat, the person who is able to get along with everyone. Why is this person not forced into one camp or the other?

The secret, of course, is that the manager/diplomat understands both points of view. This person recognizes the essential priorities of both marketing and accounting. And *you* can become that manager. It requires only that you learn how to communicate, influence, and plan with both viewpoints in mind.

THE SCOREKEEPING POINT OF VIEW

Your new, balanced focus will increase the rate of positive responses to your suggestions, as well as improve your overall management skills. To judge the degree of difference this change will make, assume the role of an executive who receives reports from a number of managers.

Most people who approach you will prepare passive reports (for example, the accountant's financial statement) and will then expect you to take some form of action or to draw a conclusion and make a decision. However, very little guidance will be provided to you, and virtually no recommendations will be given unless you ask for them. Communication commonly takes place this way.

In this exchange, however, one manager seems to have ideas for solutions. Instead of merely presenting a problem for your action, this manager suggests a course of action and supports recommendations with facts and figures. That's the manager who will get your attention every time.

Scorekeeping is a mundane function. And in the overworked accounting department, even the most capable and motivated manager might be swamped by the sheer volume of detail, often preventing execution of the prime directive of the accounting department: to interpret and then to control what's recorded.

This unfortunate situation is surpassed only by the more common problem of the accountant who has been given responsibilities beyond his or her intended role. In the typical company, top management gives the accountant many tasks that should belong to other departments. For example, Accounting prepares a budget without consulting you or it changes your initial budget. Then, during the year, you're expected to answer for unfavorable variances caused by those arbitrary changes.

The budget is a political weapon when prepared in this manner, and the situation only makes the communication gap worse than it already is. It might appear that the accounting department, in executing its budgetary role, has somehow seized political power. But the way this situation develops is far from conspiratorial. It's simply done that way when, from management's point of view, *only* the accounting department understands forecasting and the use of financial information well enough to be entrusted with the budget. Again, this belief is terribly unfair to everyone, including Accounting.

As long as management assumes Accounting is the only place to go for reliable facts, it will continue to go there. The accountant becomes the beneficiary of power and influence, wanted or unwanted. This situation comes about more from a vacuum than from a planned course of action or from a politically motivated strategy. Don't assume that accountants *want* responsibility at the level assigned; if other managers could demonstrate that they, too, can work with facts, the situation would change.

CHANGING THE SYSTEM

You can and should be responsible for any and all facts that affect your department, including the budget, the number of people you hire, the equipment and furniture you buy, and even the duties you are assigned. As long as you are accountable for the financial logic associated with decision making, decisions should not be made elsewhere.

How do you change the distribution of power and influence? By establishing and proving your ability to appreciate and address the financial side of every issue. A problem, expressed in financial terms, becomes black and white, even when the intangible elements related to that issue are gray. As a nonaccounting manager, you will prove yourself the exception to the rule, just by being able to demonstrate a financial thinking pattern.

The nonaccounting manager who is able to think and express issues in terms of cost controls, cash flow, and profits is the rare exception. Show management that you are very aware of the numbers and that you consider that awareness to be part of your job. Adopt the viewpoint that your primary duty is to save the company more money than it costs to keep you around. That's the *real* bottom line in organizational life. With that viewpoint, you cannot fail.

Be willing to demonstrate your respect for the numbers. Forget the "them and us" mentality that often prevents real communication between accountants and other managers. Always have a logical solution at hand, supported by facts that apply to the issues.

When preparing a report, ask Accounting for information. Once you have your facts on paper, consult with the accountant, asking whether your presentation is valid and whether your case can be better presented. Make use of the accounting department's experience and point of view, and think of it as your ally rather than your adversary.

ESTABLISHING COMMUNICATION

Nothing is quite as convincing as action, and you hold the power to act. The majority of unresolved conflicts remain unresolved because someone—or everyone—is unwilling to take a few simple steps to fix things.

The accounting department should provide service and cooperation to you, as long as your approach is thought out and your motives are expressed clearly. You must be prepared to act as the manager/diplomat when you approach accountants, as they might be the most defensive employees in your company. There are several reasons for this:

1. Accounting carries the burden for financial reporting that, in many cases, is neither appreciated nor shared by anyone else.
2. Accountants work with numbers to a degree that may lead you to believe that they are more comfortable with worksheets than with people.
3. The accounting department might think of itself as the company's elite. Any outside factors are perceived as unavoidable inconveniences, and the singular viewpoint becomes the only business of the company. You must be able to make your case without threatening the delicate balance of departmental self-esteem.

From this description, you may think accountants are insecure. In fact, they are no more insecure than anyone else, but their high profile in the company, often imposed by top management as a result of a broad assumption that accountants are the only reliable source for information, may make their insecurity more apparent.

Remember that having the accounting department as

an ally improves your own financial fluency. You will not have to become an accountant to improve the message you send to the top. But you will need to base your arguments in the scientific realities of company priorities. Some actions and decisions improve the bottom line, while others detract from it. An executive will consider your arguments with this fact in mind.

Example: At a meeting, you propose giving one employee a salary increase, arguing, "This employee has done a fantastic job, has mastered skills, and is now a valuable assistant." Although very positive, none of these points tells management *why* a salary increase is justified. But if you present this extremely human issue in financial terms—"This employee has become an asset to the department and is personally responsible for saving the company more than $——— over the past three months"—you take nothing away from the argument. In fact, you present the facts more clearly and specifically, and also improve your chances for approval.

Chapter 2 describes methods for translating financial information. Some of the common ratios used by accountants can help you to manage and communicate, even for nonfinancial issues.

Chapter 2

Translating Financial Information

To communicate in a numbers-oriented company, you must express your requests and conclusions in terms of financial information. Communicating financially might seem intricate and restrictive at first glance. But in fact, as every accountant knows, the trick is to simplify, to express numbers in summarized form, and to learn to explain the meaning behind the numbers.

This chapter discusses some of the analytical tools used by accountants. You will then see how the techniques can be applied and transferred to issues beyond financial concern. Because you deal in much more than numbers, you need to translate from one medium to the other—to speak the language of finance.

Example: During a meeting of department managers, one agenda item concerns staff increases. The accountant makes the point that several departments have increased their staff over the years and suggests that the coming year's budget should restrict hiring of new people. You came to the meeting intending to ask permission to hire two new employees. And you're convinced that your request is reasonable. You even believe that the new hires will be necessary and profitable. But without hard facts to back up this belief, you probably won't get your way.

Such situations are common. The accounting department draws a conclusion based on the information at hand, makes a recommendation, and wins approval. The argument is based entirely on expense reduction. You cannot argue against the accountant's recommendations unless you can present facts that prove their assumptions wrong. And that's where financial analysis becomes your best weapon.

FINANCIAL RATIOS

Accountants use ratios to explain trends and to summarize financial statements and other reports. Chances are, you will rarely use the ratios that are used in a purely financial analysis. However, by becoming familiar with the development of ratio analysis, you will be able to apply the same principles in other situations.

A ratio, by itself, is meaningless. It must be placed in a context and compared. For example, one well-known ratio is the return on sales, a comparison between net profits and total revenues expressed as a percentage. For example, a company reported gross sales of $1 million and a net profit of $70,000. The return on sales ratio is expressed as: "Last year's profits were 7 percent of sales."

What does that mean? Is 7 percent acceptable? Is it an improvement over the prior year or a severe decline? How does it compare to what was forecast twelve months earlier?

A ratio takes on meaning only when compared to a standard of some kind. Standards can include:

1. Comparison to a prior period. A ratio is compared to the same ratio for the previous year or for a series of years. Net profits are thus put into a context: "Net profits were 7 percent, compared to 6.5 percent the year before, and 4 percent the year before that."

2. Comparison to an acceptable norm. A ratio also can be compared to an industry standard, an assumed minimum, or results reported by your competitors. Example: "The 7 percent net profit last year is exceptional, considering that most companies in our industry report averages between 4 and 5 percent per year."

3. Comparison to a goal. Ratios take on the greatest significance when compared to a goal set in the past. Example: "We forecast a net profit of 5.5 percent for the year. Final results were 7 percent."

Whether you review purely financial ratios of the type that accountants use or develop your own analytical formats, always remember that significance is derived from the comparisons you draw.

Ratios are used to summarize and report what's shown on financial statements. A common failure of these reports is that ratios are simply listed, without an attempt to explain their significance. For the report to become valid and useful, the underlying trends must be explained.

Ratios are expressed in one of four ways: (1) the percentage basis we've already shown; (2) the "factor to 1" format; (3) the number of times an event occurs; (4) a single number (such as number of days, employees, or events).

Any two numbers can be expressed in one of the four ratio formats. The following examples show different expressions of the ratio relationships. Each financial ratio used by accountants answers an assumed question. You can see how ratios are developed from eight separate financial analyses (see also Figure 2-1).

1. Current ratio. Current ratio answers the question, "On average, how many dollars of assets do we have for each dollar we owe?" This question must be qualified. The word *current* refers to assets that are in the form of cash or that are readily convertible to cash (accounts receivable, securities, and inventory, for example) and to liabilities that are due and payable within twelve months.

Example: A company reports current assets of $1,825,000 and current liabilities of $892,000. The current ratio is:

$$\frac{1,825,000}{892,000} = 2.05:1$$

Figure 2-1.
Financial ratios derived from financial analyses.

current ratio	$\dfrac{\text{current assets}}{\text{current liabilities}}$	$\dfrac{1,825,000}{892,000}$ = 2.05 to 1
quick assets ratio	$\dfrac{\text{current assets less inventories}}{\text{current liabilities}}$	$\dfrac{1,214,000}{892,000}$ = 1.36 to 1
turnover in working capital	$\dfrac{\text{net sales}}{\text{current assets less current liabilities}}$	$\dfrac{7,904,000}{1,825,000 - 892,000}$ = 8.47 times
inventory turnover	$\dfrac{\text{cost of goods sold}}{\text{average inventory}}$	$\dfrac{4,754,000}{678,000}$ = 7.01 times
debt/equity ratio	$\dfrac{\text{liabilities}}{\text{tangible net worth}}$	$\dfrac{892,000}{2,031,000}$ = 4.39%
return on sales	$\dfrac{\text{net profit}}{\text{sales}}$	$\dfrac{491,000}{7,904,000}$ = 6.2%
return on capital	$\dfrac{\text{net profit}}{\text{tangible net worth}}$	$\dfrac{491,000}{2,031,000}$ = 24.2%
collection ratio	$\dfrac{\text{average accounts receivable}}{\text{average daily sales}}$	$\dfrac{972,800}{21,655}$ = 44.9 days

   2. Quick assets ratio. The quick assets ratio is similar to the current ratio but might present a more exacting test of the company's asset/liability relationship. This ratio is a comparison between current assets and current liabilities, without inventory included. The assumed question for this ratio is: "How many dollars of current assets do we have for each dollar we owe, not considering the value of inventory?"

   Example: Current assets without inventory are worth $1,214,-000, and current liabilities total $892,000. The quick assets ratio is:

$$\frac{1,214,000}{892,000} = 1.36{:}1$$

3. Turnover in working capital. This ratio compares total sales during a period (such as a full year) to working capital (the difference between current assets and current liabilities). The assumed question it answers is: "How many times, on average, did we turn over our working capital to produce the level of sales we experienced?"

Example: Net sales last year were $7,904,000. Current assets at the end of the year were $1,825,000, and current liabilities were $892,000. The turnover in working capital is:

$$\frac{7,904,000}{1,825,000 - 892,000} = 8.47 \text{ times}$$

4. Inventory turnover. This ratio compares the cost of goods sold (costs directly related to sales, such as materials purchased and direct labor) to the average inventory level. The assumed question is: "How many times, on average, did we replace our inventory during the year?"

Example: The cost of goods sold last year totaled $4,754,000, and average inventory was $678,000. The inventory turnover was:

$$\frac{\$4,754,000}{678,000} = 7.01 \text{ times}$$

5. Debt/equity ratio. This ratio is a comparison between total liabilities and tangible net worth. *Tangible* refers to net worth exclusive of assets that do not have physical value, such as covenants owned or goodwill. This ratio answers the question, "How much of our total capitalization is represented by debt?"

Example: Total liabilities equal $892,000, and the tangible net worth is $2,031,000. The debt/equity ratio is:

$$\frac{892,000}{2,031,000} = 43.9\%$$

6. *Return on sales.* This popular ratio compares the bottom-line profit with sales. It answers the question, "What percentage of total sales were retained for the period in the form of net profits?"

Example: Net profits last year were $491,000, and total sales were $7,904,000. The return on sales is:

$$\frac{491,000}{7,904,000} = 6.2\%$$

7. *Return on equity.* In this ratio, net profits are compared to shareholders' equity rather than to sales. It answers the question, "What did stockholders earn on their investment, based on net profits earned for the year?"

Example: Net profits last year totaled $491,000, and tangible net worth at the beginning of the year was $2,031,000. The return on equity is:

$$\frac{491,000}{2,031,000} = 24.2\%$$

8. *Collection ratio.* The collection ratio summarizes the trend in collections of accounts receivable. A company must monitor the time required to bring in money and determine whether their procedures are adequate and whether the trend is improving. This ratio answers the question, "On average, how many days does it take to collect an outstanding account?"

Example: Average accounts receivable last year totaled $972,800, and the average daily sales were $21,655. The collection ratio is:

$$\frac{972,800}{21,655} = 44.9 \text{ days}$$

APPLYING ANALYSIS IN YOUR DEPARTMENT

The ratios illustrated in the previous section are not meant to give you a comprehensive understanding of what accountants do when they develop tools for analysis. Neither are the precise techniques for developing averages or studying trends shown. The only purpose is to show that certain financial information is related. You can use this knowledge to devise ratios to make *your* information financially significant.

The use of ratios will improve your reporting style, enabling you to clarify the significance of information. This technique is most valuable when you are presenting a request to management. Most nonaccounting managers present less information than an executive needs to make an intelligent decision. Thus, the manager is less likely to have an idea approved.

The effect that careful analysis has can be significant. It's the difference between active and passive reporting. The passive approach is of little value, since it does not generate action. For example, you request an increase in your staffing budget. Under the passive approach, you merely point out a problem and expect management to solve it for you.

The active approach is not only more effective, it's also more useful. Instead of presenting the problem, you show how your idea will solve management's problem and make money at the same time. When making an active request, you can use the techniques of financial analysis to prove your point and to verify that your idea is, in fact, a tangible solution.

You are not restricted to using ratios for purely financial information. They are also useful for expressing a nonfinancial idea in terms familiar to executives and to accountants.

Example: You manage a department that processes a large volume of transactions. You plan to ask for a staff increase. Your staff has not grown sufficiently over the last three years, even though the transaction load, in your opinion, has probably doubled during that time. To support your request, you originally planned to make the point that your staff is overworked and is running behind deadlines. But using the techniques of trend analysis, you determine that a better approach is to study and report the volume of transactions over the last five years. This is an example of using a financial technique to report on a nonfinancial issue.

In your opinion, you have made your department more efficient over time. You suspect that employees are handling more transactions now than they did five years ago. But you cannot go to the budget meeting with only a hunch, so you go back over your records and determine that the volume of transactions has more than doubled during the last five years. Your staff has grown from four people at the beginning of that period to eight people today, and you want to add two more employees during the coming year. You could simply request an increase in the budget. But chances are, you will be turned down. For lack of a solution, management might decide to not address the problem you present.

Turning instead to trend analysis, you list the yearly transactions for the five-year period. You then list the average number of employees in the department each year. Dividing the transactions processed by the number of employees, you arrive at a ratio, representing the transactions processed per employee. Overall, the number of transactions per employee has risen during the period, a sign that efficiency has grown during the five years. Figure 2-2 summarizes this information.

Figure 2-2.
Trend analysis showing ratio of the number of transactions per employee.

YEAR	YEARLY TRANSACTIONS	NUMBER OF EMPLOYEES	RATIO
1	24,711	4	6,178
2	35,192	5	7,038
3	35,810	5	7,162
4	46,791	7	6,684
5	57,844	8	7,231

What is the value of this brief report? It anticipates and offsets the argument that hiring more employees is not justified. It is very frustrating to attend a meeting and make a request, only to be turned down for the wrong reasons. A possible response is, "You've already doubled the size of your staff. Instead of hiring more people, why don't you make the process more efficient?" This report shows that you've already done that. It justifies the request by the fact that (1) the load of transactions has grown and probably will continue to grow, and (2) you're processing work more efficiently now than five years ago. By summarizing a trend, you answer the questions that might arise during a budget meeting, the most important of which is: "Why should we let this manager increase the staff level?"

To emphasize the improved efficiency in your department, summarize the transactions processed per employee on a graph for the five-year period as shown in Figure 2-3. Graphic summaries help bring your report—and your argument—to life. When information is presented visually, it is comprehended more quickly, and you will be more likely to win approval of your request.

BEING AWARE OF CULTURAL AND POLITICAL DIFFERENCES

Summarizing trends by correctly reporting the real facts— and not the assumed source of savings—helps you to win your point, because the real issues can then be addressed. Requests and ideas that will be approved share common attributes:

1. They are clearly presented.
2. They will produce profits or reduce costs, or if costs are increased, those increases are justified by volume and profit growth.
3. They are presented by managers who also present solutions.

Accountants, who are in the verification and financial business, are accustomed to presenting information that has

Figure 2-3.
Sample graphic summary.

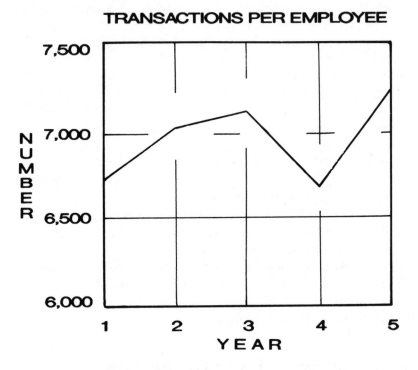

these attributes. In comparison, managers who deal more with people and less with numbers have a more difficult time addressing the issues to which top management is likely to respond. It's not that department and division managers are not concerned with profits—chances are, they are constantly aware of the profit issue. But in the form of communication used, the accountant is more at home with the numbers.

This disparity between accounting and nonaccounting managers results in cultural and political divisions within the company. Because the financially aware accountant probably gains influence in the eyes of top management, the accounting department and its manager often are at the focal point of decision making. The president and other top executives are under pressure to produce profits, to improve efficiency, and to explain any shortcomings to the stockholders or to a board of directors. Therefore the accounting department becomes a valuable resource for dependable information.

If you want to contribute something of value, developing the same communication skills is essential. Taking a passive approach to internal communication is a risky, if not a helpless, posture. To avoid becoming a voiceless, helpless victim of the ruling corporate culture, you must arm yourself with facts.

Accountants know how to present information so that management can make decisions based on tangible issues. If they want to increase their staff, they know how to present a case proving that an increase is essential. If they need more floor space, they are able to prove that the company will benefit by granting the request.

There is nothing dishonest or unethical about presenting information so that you win approval, and there is nothing wrong in the approach that accountants take to gain approval. In fact, preparing facts that make decisions easy is every manager's job.

Consider it *your* job to advise top management. You are the expert in your department, and you know better than anyone else how to solve the problems you face.

ACCURACY IN FINANCIAL REPORTING

When the accounting department is given the final word, it's not always fair, but it will happen unless you're prepared to speak in terms of facts and figures. Accountants are not experts in the issues of your department; they only know about the numbers. And as you know, the numbers do not always tell the whole story. Even worse, the numbers can be distorted—even unintentionally—so that the conclusion drawn is the exact opposite of the truth.

Example: You are the head of a sales department, supervising twenty-two commissioned people. Your budget for the coming year includes commissions, travel, entertainment, and related expenses. You are asking for a larger budget than the year before.

Your initial budget simply lists the monthly expenses you expect to see, and you did not supply any supporting facts. The budget is presented to the accounting department for review. During the next meeting, the accountant recommends cutting back on your request, and justifies the recommendation by pointing out that the average cost per employee has risen over the last four years.

If you are a passive manager, this would be the end of the discussion. It's difficult to argue with facts. The accountant's report points out an apparent control problem: You are not holding expenses at a "reasonable" level, a conclusion honestly reached with the facts at hand. So management will decide to restrict your budget and force you to watch expenses more carefully.

As an active manager aware of how to use trend analysis, you know that the story does not end with average cost. You also know how to present the full facts so that management will be able to make an informed decision. Costs per employee have been rising, but you also know that gross profit has been increasing as well. Figure 2-4 shows the accountant's report (Analysis A) and your report (Analysis B).

Analysis A appears to show a very negative trend. But Analysis B shows the full picture: costs, sales, and profits. Even with increased per-employee costs, the gross profit has been growing.

TRENDS AND STANDARDS

Translating financial information with the full facts, and explaining those facts to management, is only one way to use the techniques of financial analysis. You can also use these techniques to set standards in your department. Your task as a leader is to motivate employees to attain a standard for quality and timeliness. Perhaps most of all, you want to help people to achieve their personal and career goals. In one respect, the company exists to provide this benefit to its employees. And in that respect, your job is to help employees to succeed.

Figure 2-4.
Accurate trend reporting.

ANALYSIS A

cost per employee

YEAR	EMPLOYEES	TOTAL COST	AVERAGE COST
1	11	$32,612	$2,965
2	13	40,501	3,115
3	17	56,288	3,311
4	22	78,406	3,564

ANALYSIS B

production versus cost

YEAR	TOTAL COST	GROSS SALES	GROSS PROFIT	EMPLOYEES	AVERAGE PER EMPLOYEE
1	$32,612	$64,843	$32,231	11	$2,930
2	40,501	79,518	39,017	13	3,001
3	56,288	117,604	61,316	17	3,607
4	78,406	168,202	89,796	22	4,082

Setting standards for performance is not always a simple task. On an assembly line, each employee is expected to complete a minimum number of defect-free units per shift, and performance is measured on that basis. But in an office or within a service organization, a precise standard for judging performance is harder to define.

That's where the techniques used in financial analysis can be used. They can be applied to people and to performance, as well as to numbers. Your challenge is to arrive at a specific, tangible method for judgment. The problem is that you don't necessarily produce a product that can be examined for quality. How can you translate a "numbers" technique to define performance?

Example: At the beginning of a review period, you meet with each employee in your department to define a mutually acceptable goal. It might be as simple as completing a number of transactions per month, reducing errors, or meeting specified deadlines. Or it might be as complicated as attaining higher skill levels or mastering complex systems. Regardless of the goal, it must be specific. And it must have a deadline.

One of your employees is a computer operator who is responsible for inputting transactions to an automated system. You and the employee agree that during the next six months, the average monthly transactions processed will increase from 5,500 to 6,500 per month, the average number that other departmental employees process. In addition, the employee agrees to set the goal of mastering techniques for investigating and correcting errors.

You prepare a trend chart like the one shown in Figure 2-5, which shows the acceptable range of transactions to be processed each month during the period (the shaded area) and also tracks the actual number processed. This chart should be updated by the employee so that actual progress toward the goal can be visualized.

The manager/diplomat will be able to instill such an idea without posing a threat to an employee. That's a leadership skill, and nothing more. If you have an employee who is not performing at par, you must be able to precisely define the problem and to help the employee devise a way to solve

Figure 2-5.
Trend standards.

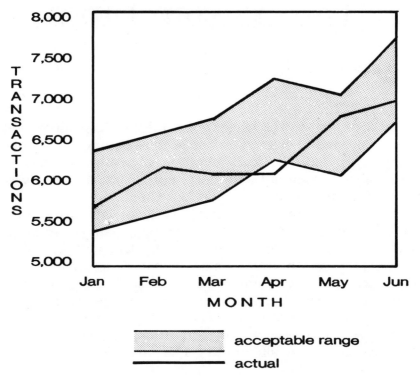

acceptable range

actual

it. By providing a reasonable and precise goal, you help people achieve positive results.

In this example, financial analysis is given an added dimension. It becomes a tool for leading people, not just for manipulating numbers. This use of financial analysis might be the best possible, since it helps employees achieve personal security and self-esteem, a sense of accomplishment, and definition of their own performance. When your department's "product" is intangible, you add a valuable service by defining goals and having a way to measure success.

Chapter 3 examines the meaning of profit and the different ways that ratios and trends are used to bring the numbers to life.

Chapter 3

The Bottom Line

To an accountant, "the bottom line" means the profit earned during the year. For the purpose of this chapter that definition is expanded: The bottom line means getting the answers you need and want, all with the use of the financial analysis techniques discussed in the previous chapter.

The accountant's "product" is financial information that is arranged, recorded, interpreted, and reported to stockholders, the board of directors, lenders, and other employees. But your bottom line involves human resources and the production and completion of tasks. An accountant is concerned with profit and yield; you look for quality and timely completion of work. An accountant seeks solutions to cash flow problems and return on investment; you seek better ways to do your job and to get the most from the people you supervise.

YOUR EXPERT STATUS

Just as the accountant is an expert in the numbers of the company, you are the expert in your area of responsibility. You cannot avoid confronting the financial issues of management; that's part of your environment and culture. But the alienation between accountants and nonaccounting managers revolves around differences in viewpoint.

This chapter shows how to achieve several important goals:

Apply ratio and trend analysis in a nonaccounting environment. Accountants approach financial questions and translate numbers into ratios and then express their significance within a continuing trend. This chapter tells how the same approach can be used in a nonfinancial situation.

Transfer the techniques used to study profitability to solve nonfinancial problems. Accounting techniques can be applied to a broad range of subjects. The value of these techniques for the nonaccounting manager is in devising ways to clarify otherwise intangible points. The accountant deals with tangible facts—profit and loss, volume, cash flow, and measurement of documented results against a clear standard (the budget). Your problems may be less tangible. You will see how any problem in your department can be made tangible enough to evaluate, so that commonsense solutions can be arrived at and tracked.

Improve communication skills through the use of financial techniques. Measuring results—notably in your nonfinancial environment—is a difficult task. If you change a procedure, how do you tell whether your change was better or worse? How can you evaluate employee performance, quality of work, or relative productivity? All of these items can be measured, but only when you reduce your analysis to a measurable factor.

Many nonaccounting managers experience anxiety about their qualifications to use financial skills in a constructive manner. You are not trained or experienced in the skills that accountants demonstrate in meetings, reports, and verbal presentations. If you do suffer from the math or qualification anxiety so common among managers, take heart. You can overcome that point of view and adopt a fresh approach.

Consider these facts:

- You *are* the expert in your department.
- You will be able to apply techniques used by accountants in communicating facts about numbers to solve the less tangible but equally important problems you face every day.
- You will improve your effectiveness and leadership

success by learning to view every problem not just as a problem, but also as an opportunity to arrive at a solution.

Once you can accept and believe these ideas, you will be well on your way toward mastering the secrets used by accountants. Most of the task involves attitude and anxiety about skill levels. We all know that a problem can be solved once it's defined. That's why the techniques of financial analysis are so valuable to you.

DEFINING YIELD

To an accountant, "yield" is the production of profit from investing (or spending) money or from creating sales in a particular market or product line. The word *yield* might be used interchangeably with *return, net profit,* or *gain,* depending on the circumstances. We are not as concerned with the accounting definition, however, as we are with identifying the yield you expect to realize from activities within your own department.

Example: The manager of a data processing department is given the assignment of ensuring accurate and efficient processing. That means developing input, processing, and output procedures within a budget; training employees in many departments to use terminals; and coordinating schedules and priorities. All of these processes translate to forms of yield.

The manager is concerned with work yield from employees in the data processing department; with output yield of printed reports; and with the yield from internal training. If these tasks are well defined and approached properly, then standards can be set. And once a standard is set, it can be measured.

Accountants precisely follow this procedure with the numbers. They define yearly income, cost and expense goals;

they determine responsibility for meeting those goals; and they measure success through the budget.

Having made a task measurable, the next step is to interpret results. Is a current trend positive or negative, and why? Do results fall within an acceptable range? And how can the process be improved beyond its current status? Of greater urgency is the problem that you may misinterpret information. Even if you know what is significant, how can you judge what constitutes a positive result?

Every analyst, including the accountant, faces this problem, even when dealing with tangible and universally understood ideas about yield. Arriving at accurate answers is only part of the solution. Interpreting those results correctly is where you really roll up your sleeves and get to work.

Example: Profits increased over a four-year period in your company in a range starting at $72,000 and ending at $83,000. At first glance, this trend appears to be positive. But when those profits are reviewed as the percentage of yield on stockholders' equity, a different trend emerges.

The company has raised new capital during the four-year period with the idea of expanding markets. An analysis of net profits appeared to prove that in fact, this had been achieved. But further review showed declining net profit yield as Figure 3-1 illustrates.

Figure 3-1.
Yield comparisons.

YEAR	AVERAGE CAPITAL	NET PROFIT AMOUNT	%
1	$535,000	$72,000	13.5%
2	685,000	75,000	10.9
3	815,000	78,000	9.6
4	980,000	83,000	8.5

FINDING THE SIGNIFICANCE

Analysis is not merely concerned with putting numbers on paper and then developing a ratio. A trend could be negative because the percentage of profit is declining in relation to average capital. But the trend might still be called positive if a case could be made for the cost of investing in expansion.

If the additional capital had been used to open new offices and hire and train sales representatives and then to add overhead to support new markets, the decline in net profits might be completely justified. The argument could be made that future profits will be greater due to expansion costs this year, but that required investing new capital to create the market.

So the question of interpretation goes beyond the obvious black and white of the numbers. That's where the traditional accounting department analysis fails in many cases. If Accounting is given the task of reporting and interpreting the financial trends in the case above, what conclusion should it draw?

There is no absolute answer to this question, because *the problem has not yet been defined.* You cannot draw an informed conclusion without consulting the right experts. For the accountant to understand the significance of this trend, it will first be necessary to confer with Marketing to examine the components of costs and expenses that reduced the yield and to anticipate what they mean for the future.

The same problem will arise in your analysis of yield as it applies to the nonfinancial problems in your department. If employees are more productive this year than last year, or if the number of transactions processed is growing, what does that mean? You might discover that to report information accurately, it is necessary to first consult with experts: your own employees, managers of other departments, or the accounting department.

The point to be made about analysis is this: The belief that accountants possess some magic information not available to the rest of us is a myth. They are trained in the skill of reducing numbers to meaningful fact. But if they do not research beyond the mere numbers, they are likely to draw the wrong conclusions. All managers can learn from this, by realizing that it's not just the numbers that have meaning; you must look beyond, ask questions, and develop the best possible opinions based on a fair evaluation of different points of view.

COMPARING LIKE INFORMATION

Analysis depends on drawing conclusions from comparison. Thus, two or more sets of fact must be reviewed together and must have a relationship that affects the trend under study. Seemingly related information will not necessarily be comparable because of differences in the time periods involved, or in outside factors, such as markets, locations, or product costs.

Example: Your company is split into two divisions. One sells products, and the other markets services. The yield in the service division is much higher than that in the product division. But because the structure of the financial makeup in each division is so different, a comparison of yields is meaningless.

Example: The yield from activity in one region is much higher than that in another. One possible conclusion is that the profitable region is run more efficiently. But an investigation reveals that the competition is much stronger in the second region. A surface comparison does not reveal this fact.

Example: Two similar departments in one company are compared during a budget review. The first has had the same number of employees for the past five years, while the second has doubled its staff size. Does this mean the manager of the second department is less efficient or less effective? Or does the change reflect the type of work being processed, the applicability of automated systems to the first department, or the change in demand on the departments?

It is a mistake to believe that financial analysis is a quick cure. The numbers often tell only a small part of the whole story. Depending only on the numbers is a mistake often made by accountants and nonaccountants alike. Over-dependence on just the numbers will cloud judgment and prevent you from arriving at the right conclusion.

Accountants compare the bottom line between periods. A return on sales that's isolated only to the high-volume summer months cannot be compared to a full year, when average volume is much lower. And for investors, a short-term profit is not the same as a long-term profit of the same percentage.

To see how this works, compare different investment profits by dividing the profit by the basis (the purchase price adjusted for any costs of purchase).

Example: A company invested available cash in four different se-curities. Each was held for a different period of time. To determine relative profitability, all must be compared on a like basis. Because the holding period was different, profits must be expressed so that the average annual profit can be reported accurately.

The four investments were:

Basis	Months held	Profit	Percentage
$ 5,000	16	$ 650	13.00%
8,000	20	900	11.25
12,000	4	300	2.50
15,000	8	1,200	8.00

At first glance, it appears that the most profitable investment was the $15,000 (based on the amount of profit) or the $5,000 (based on the percentage of profit). But to make a valid comparison, the yield must be expressed correctly: How much profit was earned during the av-erage 12-month period?

Figure 3-2 shows the correct annualized profit for each of the four investments. The results are much different from those shown in the table above. The figure also shows the steps involved in annu-alizing a yield.

Being able to express yield in consistent terms is an im-portant skill. If your information is to be reliable, it must

Figure 3-2.
Annualized return.

BASIS	PROFIT	MONTHS HELD	ANNUALIZED YIELD
$ 5,000	$ 650	16	9.75%
8,000	900	20	6.75
12,000	300	4	7.50
15,000	1,200	8	12.00

STEPS

1. $$\frac{\text{profit}}{\text{basis}} = \text{yield}$$

2. $$\frac{\text{yield}}{\text{months held}} = \text{monthly yield}$$

3. $$\text{monthly yield} \times 12 = \text{annualized yield}$$

also be comparable. Remember that management does not think in terms of individual departmental cycles but in terms of *annual* return on investment or sales. For example, you might be very aware that a high-volume summer season is the most critical period for your department. Your point of view could be restricted to that period. But management is probably more concerned with the annual expense or profit you and other departments experienced.

The techniques for expressing dollar amounts of profit on an annualized basis can be applied to nonfinancial situations. For example, you are reporting on the trend in the number of transactions your department handles. That number grows substantially in July, August, and September and then falls off for the rest of the year. It might be more appropriate to prepare your report with the entire year in mind rather than emphasizing just the busiest time of the year.

Expressing information on a consistent basis shows that even an apparently simple black-and-white comparison might have complications. A good analyst is not one who is comfortable with numbers and who understands how to manipulate or summarize them. A truly good analyst is one who understands the real issues beyond those numbers, who knows how to get to the heart of the issue, even if the numbers look like the whole story to everyone else.

A good analyst is careful in the selection of facts, financial or otherwise, making sure that all of the factors in the comparison are for the correct time periods, that they are related to one another, and that a valid comparison can be made. Some examples will help to show how this financial principle can be applied in different, nonfinancial situations.

Example: A purchasing manager studies the number of completed orders processed by employees in her department for the first quarter and compares the results to the full previous year. She concludes that productivity in her department is falling. But further analysis shows that purchasing activity is much greater than average during the peak summer months. A comparison to the previous year's first quarter reveals a slight improvement in actual productivity.

Example: A shipping manager tracks the average time required to complete orders, from the time a requisition is received until goods are delivered to the customer. Over a period of several months, the average time has declined, which appears to be a positive trend. The analysis would usually stop there. But the manager considers another factor: Shipping and receiving staff increased by 30 percent during the time in question. So the manager concluded that there was no basis for a comparison. The environment had changed, so the previous trend was invalidated.

Example: An accountant recommends cutting the travel budget for the marketing department, based on a trend toward increased expenses per sale. The analysis carefully compared gross profit and volume to expense levels and made a strong case for reducing the budget. However, the marketing manager pointed out that the company was offering different product lines than in the past and explained that selling the new products required more travel, because of higher customer service needs after the sale. Thus, the trend could not be applied to activities involving the new product line.

In each of these cases, an apparent conclusion turned out to be wrong when more information was taken into consideration. Informed, correct decisions can be made only when the facts are used appropriately. These examples point out a flaw often present in analysis: Many conclusions as drawn are simply incorrect, because the wrong facts are used or because some facts are left out. The information is not inaccurate, but a body of correct information led the analyst to the wrong answer.

APPLYING TRENDS

A body of facts that goes into the process of drawing a conclusion must be validated. This validation requires using expertise, tapping resources both in and out of your department, and seeking constructive criticism.

Ratios, like those used by accountants for financial reporting, can be developed for other purposes as well and provide excellent reporting summaries for any manager. To correctly place information within a trend, you must address two problems. First, the information must be valid in order for the conclusion to make sense. And second, both the ratio and the underlying trend must be appropriate and meaningful.

Example: A manager takes great pains to investigate his facts, making certain they're comparable and that they can be compared. But in reporting on the trend, he does not know whether that trend is positive or negative.

If your conclusions are to be useful, you must be able to interpret the results of trend analysis. An accountant will know what gross and net profit trends mean to the company. And you possess the same type of knowledge about information related to your department, assuming you select information in a relevant manner.

Example: A manager prepares a report showing the trend in employee workload. Her purpose is to request a higher staffing budget and more floor space. However, the analysis shows the increasing trend in staff and floor space on a companywide basis. It is not unique to her department and cannot be used to support her case.

Example: An accountant points to unfavorable results in budgeted variable expenses (expenses whose levels are affected to a degree by sales volume) in the marketing department. However, the forecast sales are also well above the forecast level, so the *overall* trend is a favorable one. It's not reasonable to accept a favorable sales variance and still find fault with related but unfavorable expense variances.

Many forms of analysis lose their significance because they are not interpreted in one of the two appropriate ways: progressively or within an acceptable range. A progressive trend is expected to change over time. Examples include the dollar volume of gross sales. A flat trend could be positive if you first define what is an "acceptable" range. A trend, even a declining one, may not even indicate a problem, if the results exceeded a specific goal.

Example: A marketing manager sets the goal that the average newly recruited salesperson shall make no fewer than twenty new contacts per month. As long as each person reaches that goal, they are performing to standard. It would be unreasonable, however, to say the trend is negative if one salesperson contacts forty people one month but only twenty-five the month after. That's not a decline in productivity; it still falls within the defined acceptable range.

Example: A company is expected to earn at least 12 percent net profit each year. In three years, actual net profits are 13, 15, and 12 percent. Does the third year reflect a deterioration in the trend? No, as long as profits meet or exceed the reasonable standard that has been set. It would be unrealistic to expect a trend of this nature to continue to improve each year.

When you follow a trend in your department, decide whether your standard is for an ever-growing result or for results falling within a range. The differences between the two types of positive trends are shown in Figure 3-3.

Figure 3-3(a) shows tracking of an increasing trend over time. If the line begins to fall, a negative change is indicated.

Example: The branch manager of an insurance company tracks the total number of policies sold per year. The trend is positive as long as the salesforce continues producing more business.

Figure 3-3(b) specifies a range of acceptable results and then tracks actual results. The idea is that with proper management, results can be controlled to remain within the boundaries.

Example: The collection department manager wants to collect all outstanding bills within forty-five days from billing date. When this range is exceeded, they become problem accounts. Realistically, the average is not expected to ever fall below thirty days. So the trend cannot be progressive; there are natural limits to the results.

PUTTING TRENDS TO WORK

The following is a step-by-step process in which the principles of trend analysis are applied. The first step is the discovery of a problem, followed by identification of the best solution, including a determination of facts that must be used in that process.

Example: As manager of a software development company's customer service department, you believe complaints are on the increase.

Figure 3-3.
Positive trends.

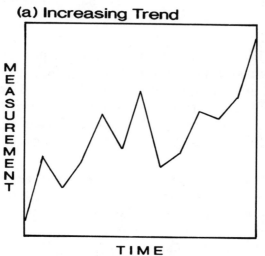

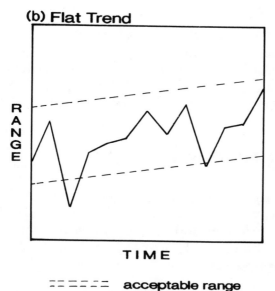

You think most such problems are in the technical support and service areas. This suspicion, though, is not enough to *prove* the cause. In order to get approval for action, the problem must be proved.

Trend analysis helps to make this point. So you break down the types of calls your department received during the past year as Figure 3-4 shows.

Your task is now to determine whether a predictable relationship can be found between the rising level of complaint calls and the large volume of technical and service requests. You suspect that this is the case. So you prepare charts for technical and service requests and for complaints, as shown in Figure 3-5.

These charts demonstrate a similar curve of customer calls within recent months, but the information is inconclusive. It could be argued that complaint calls are the result of increased volume. You need to take a different approach.

The next step is to compare the number of technical and service calls with complaints and develop a ratio to see whether the volume

Figure 3-4.
Sample trend analysis worksheet.

Type of Contact

	New Product Inquiries	Product Upgrade Inquiries	Technical Requests	Service Requests	Complaints
January	310	46	1,050	780	17
February	207	52	1,660	1,020	26
March	384	41	1,220	830	19
April	115	44	2,010	1,420	18
May	305	56	1,430	1,300	41
June	288	37	1,880	1,540	52
July	412	42	2,190	2,010	137
August	399	40	2,280	2,640	120
September	429	41	2,860	2,730	161
October	380	37	2,470	2,240	176
November	307	30	2,220	2,810	189
December	329	38	1,960	2,900	232

Figure 3-5.
Charts showing customer service trends.

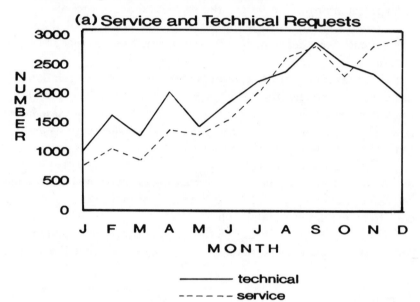

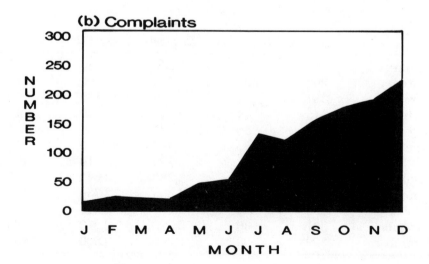

Figure 3-6.
Sample worksheet comparing service calls and customer complaints.

Month	Technical Requests	Service Requests	Month	Complaints
Jan	1,050	780	Feb	26
Feb	1,660	1,020	Mar	19
Mar	1,220	830	Apr	18
Apr	2,010	1,420	May	41
May	1,430	1,300	Jun	52
Jun	1,880	1,540	Jul	137
Jul	2,190	2,010	Aug	120
Aug	2,880	2,640	Sep	161
Sep	2,860	2,730	Oct	176
Oct	2,470	2,240	Nov	189
Nov	2,220	2,810	Dec	232

of complaints is growing at a greater rate than the trend in other types of calls.

You make one assumption at this point: If complaints are related to technical and service calls, the complaints should be expected about one month after the problem occurs. Thus, technical and service calls are compared with complaints for the following month. From the worksheet (Figure 3-6), you can develop a ratio showing the relationship between technical and service requests and complaints showing up a month later.

The complaint ratio is summarized in Figure 3-7.

Your case is now well established. The ratio of complaints has risen over the course of the year, strongly supporting your contention. The argument in this case can be made even stronger by visual presentation. So as a final step in your report, you prepare a graph as shown in Figure 3-8.

The problem in this case was to establish and then support the idea that a negative trend was under way. That problem was resolved by using the techniques of financial analysis.

Figure 3-7.
Complaint ratios.

COMPLAINT MONTH	1 *	2 **
February	.025	.033
March	.011	.019
April	.015	.022
May	.020	.029
June	.036	.040
July	.073	.089
August	.055	.060
September	.056	.061
October	.062	.064
November	.077	.084
December	.105	.083

$$* \ 1 = \frac{\text{complaint}}{\text{technical requests}}$$

$$** \ 2 = \frac{\text{complaint}}{\text{service requests}}$$

The ability to correctly study information and draw a constructive conclusion, is a skill that every manager wants. Information can be interpreted in a number of ways; in fact, the same body of "facts" might lead two managers to opposite conclusions. The solution is to first understand exactly what problem is involved and to then verify that the facts

Figure 3-8.
Complaint trends.

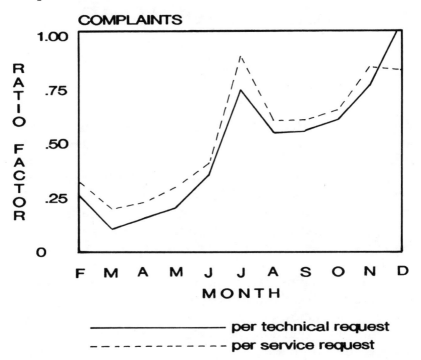

used to study a trend do, indeed, apply to the problem. Do those facts present the information that tells you whether the trend is positive or negative? Do the facts relate to the trend under discussion? And how does the collection of facts help you to identify the actions that should be taken to correct the problem? These questions are essential to ask.

Chapter 4

Cost Allocation

One function within the accounting discipline is cost allocation, the assignment of costs to divisions or departments within a company. Cost allocation is essential and revealing in a manufacturing environment, where different production cost centers should be compared and judged. But the practice of allocating in nonmanufacturing situations often is misguided and taken to an extreme. Still, many companies allow or even expect the accountant to go through the exercise.

This chapter explains the principles of cost allocation and demonstrates the appropriate applications of that discipline. It then shows how the idea often is applied to other areas and how that affects you as a manager. Finally, you will see how to challenge an arbitrary allocation made to your department and how you can use allocation techniques to improve your own management skills.

COST AND PROFIT CENTERS

The accountant's world would be ideal if all the money a company spent could be scientifically linked to one department or division. But a brief review of the nature of expenses shows that this cannot be done.

Example: Your company has eleven departments, each with its own annual budget. It is a simple matter to determine each department's telephone, salary, and employee benefit expenses, as they are identified quickly, easily, and specifically. But such expenses as rent, utilities, and building maintenance apply to the company as a whole and cannot be broken down specifically by department.

Because general expenses are by nature not applicable to any one department, any allocation must be arbitrary. No attempt to make a random allocation fair and equitable will offset this reality. And even if expenses are assigned to every department, the exercise is not useful because not every department has a direct relationship to the generation of income.

Since many departments do not directly generate income, cost allocation results in no meaningful information on which management can act. With that in mind, you should ask yourself, *Since cost allocation provides nothing of value, why is it done?* This is not just a rhetorical question. It's one that should be asked in every nonmanufacturing company, and it should be asked frequently. The only honest answer is that it should not be done when it provides no value.

Accountants recognize profit centers, places where income is produced or generated. For example, in a manufacturing plant, three separate divisions create finished goods from raw materials. These products are then sold to customers. In this situation, all of the costs and expenses of a division can be linked directly to sales and should be accounted for separately. Only in that way is it possible to know whether a product is produced and sold at a profit.

The attempt to apply these principles in an administrative environment, such as a support department in a service organization, is futile and meaningless. A support department does not create product or directly provide service to a customer. So assigning broad expenses on a departmental basis gives no guidance to management.

Example: The accountant presents a monthly report, which includes a comment that the purchasing department has exceeded its budget for building maintenance. What does this tell management? What can be done to correct the problem? Or, more to the point, what's the problem? It certainly is not that the purchasing department is spending excessive money repairing the building; the problem is that meaningless allocations are being made.

When a department or a division does generate gross income, the applicable costs and expenses can be broken down and assigned. But when a department does not participate in the direct production of income, there is no purpose in doing this, other than to satisfy an accounting convention or to satisfy management that somewhere, somehow, an effort is being made to analyze expenses in as much detail as possible.

Example: An insurance company contracts with independent agencies for the sale of policies. In the home office, several distinct departments exist: underwriting, claims, policyowner service, marketing, commission accounting, premium accounting, general accounting, personnel, data processing, and the executive offices. None of these departments is directly involved in the production of income (that is handled solely through the agency system). Yet, the accounting department assigns all costs and expenses on a departmental basis each month.

To demonstrate how meaningless this exercise is, consider these facts:

- All income is assigned to the marketing department, whereas all commission expenses are slotted in the commission accounting department.
- Each department is assigned a portion of fixed overhead expense, although none generates income.
- Although allocated expenses are compared to departmental budgets, variances cannot be acted upon, because breakdowns are arbitrary and beyond the control of department managers.

The last point is critical. Why are costs assigned to a department if the responsible manager of that department cannot affect or control the amount of money spent? Allocation should be made for the purpose of meaningful analysis and control and for nothing less.

Defining and recognizing cost and profit sources is important when divisions have responsibility for generating income. But when it comes to support functions, cost allocation does not belong.

TRACING DIRECT COSTS

Later in this chapter, you'll see how cost allocation can be put into practical use in your department. For now, let's review how costs are traced by income-producing divisions and what the results reveal.

A *direct cost* is an expenditure that is directly related to the production of income. For example, materials are purchased, marked up, and sold; or wages are paid to people who manufacture product from raw materials. *Gross profit* is the amount left over when direct costs are deducted from sales.

The costs of a manufacturing or income-producing division determines profitability. So a cost accountant gives management needed information for comparing one product line to another.

Example: A company produces one product but has three regional manufacturing plants. Each division is analyzed and compared monthly, and a report is prepared showing relative costs. Keeping in mind that each plant is producing the same product, the costs should be approximately the same for each division each month. Of course, this assumption must be modified because of regional cost variances. For example, in one part of the country, materials and labor are more expensive than in another. And in one region, facility rent is much higher than the average.

Figure 4-1 shows a typical monthly summary.

The gross profit for divisions 1 and 3 are about the same; however, division 2 reports a substantially lower gross profit. This may be caused by a combination of factors, such as:

Figure 4-1.
Cost comparisons.

	DIVISION 1	DIVISION 2	DIVISION 3
gross sales	$845,960	$610,405	$932,008
direct costs	491,315	407,211	539,914
gross profit	$354,645	$203,194	$392,094
	41.9%	33.3%	42.1%

- Costs may be higher when sales are lower.
- The cost of doing business in that region—including material and labor costs—may be higher than in the other regions.
- Production methods may be less efficient or poorly managed.
- Special problems may be encountered in division 2, such as more frequent breakdowns of older machinery, local competition for a limited labor force, or localized labor problems.

All of these possibilities must be evaluated for management to draw a correct conclusion. In one company, the president attended a meeting and read the accountant's unfavorable report on a branch office in the Northeast. He was planning to close the office because winter production was far below expectations until he spoke with the branch office vice-president and discovered that particularly harsh weather had prevented delivery of raw materials.

Not everything management needs to know can be discovered in reports. It's usually necessary to speak with people to get the real facts; the numbers are only guidelines smart managers use to decide which questions to ask.

If the margin of gross profit is consistently lower for division 2, it might be necessary to close the plant and concentrate production in the other two divisions. But in deciding this, management must consider other factors:

Capacity in the other plants may be limited, so that they won't be able to absorb the added volume.

The cost of getting finished products to the market may be high enough to justify keeping the less profitable division in operation.

The cost breakdown might include costs or expenses that will continue whether the plant is left open or closed. In that case, profitability in the remaining divisions would be affected.

As you can see, drawing a definite conclusion from the numbers alone is not simple. The different results may be caused by many factors, and those causes must be understood. Then, before deciding upon the correct action, management must realize the consequences. The complexities of interpretation go beyond the numbers. Because they deal with numbers so extensively, some accountants fall into the trap of believing that financial information tells the whole story. That is rarely the case.

EXPENSE ALLOCATIONS

In a strictly manufacturing environment, allocation often extends beyond direct costs. The cost accountant breaks down all expenses by division as well, and often in great detail. That process enables the accountant to arrive at a net profit for each operating group.

Expense allocations in that situation may be proper and justified because each division directly participates in profit generation and because management needs to assess profitability. That assessment can be applied not only on the basis of gross profit, but all the way to the bottom line.

Example: A manufacturing company has three divisions. The cost allocation procedure calls for breakdowns of all costs and expenses on a direct basis. Each cost is traced specifically by division. And overhead expenses are assigned to a division on one of several logical tests:

Percentage of gross sales. Some expenses are divided based on total volume, such as administrative salaries and benefits, home office delivery expenses, dues and subscriptions, and general repairs and maintenance. Closely related to this method is the breakdown of costs based on units a division produces each month.

Direct allocation. By tracking requisitions, the accounting department assigns office supply expenses directly to each division. And the telephone bill is broken down by extension, so that expense can also be allocated directly.

Square footage. Some expenses, such as rent, utilities, and insurance, are allocated on the basis of square feet occupied by each division. The justification is that these expenses vary by space usage.

Even distribution. Certain categories of expense cannot be equitably divided and would not vary if additional plants were opened or existing plants were closed. These are allocated one-third to each division.

An example of how expense allocations are computed is shown in Figure 4-2. In this example, three types of overhead expense are assigned on the basis of square footage in each division. Each month, the total expense is broken down and allocated by applying the proportional square footage and then assigning the expense on the same basis. So if one division expands its factory area, it would be allocated a higher amount. That is fair, in that each type of expense would increase directly due to expansion.

In the event of expansion, it must be assumed that more space increases the capacity for production of gross income. Thus, allocation on a square-foot basis is appropriate for many categories of expense. But the key here is that the relationship between income on the one hand and costs and expenses on the other, is specific and direct. If your department does not produce income directly, you should not be made responsible for allocated expenses you cannot control.

THE FIXED OVERHEAD PROBLEM

When overhead expenses are described as "fixed," that can mean two things. To most accountants, a fixed expense is one

Figure 4-2.
Expense allocation based on square footage.

	DIVISION 1	DIVISION 2	DIVISION 3
total square feet=32,600	10,400	8,200	14,000
	31.9%	25.2%	42.9%
rent	$26,158	$20,664	$35,178
utilities	2,951	2,331	3,968
insurance	11,101	8,770	14,929

allocations

total expense	
rent	$82,000
utilities	9,250
insurance	34,800

that does not vary with changes in sales volume. For example, a contractual rent expense is fixed for a period of time and will not change even if gross sales double.

A second definition of fixed expenses is that they are permanent. Using the example of rent, it is fixed because the company will always need space. This second meaning of "fixed" overhead raises an issue that often is overlooked in the evaluation of profit and loss.

Example: A company runs four divisions and evaluates profit and loss every month. Divisions 1, 3, and 4 earn an average of 42 percent gross profit and, after expenses, net profits of approximately 6 percent each year. But division 2 grosses only 33 percent and has reported net losses for the past four years. Fixed overhead has been allocated to each division on a combination of assumptions, including square footage, sales volume, and equal sharing.

Management determines that division 2 is losing money and should be closed down. However, a comparison of the latest year's results reveals that the losing division absorbs expenses, and therefore should be left open:

Allocation with four divisions

	Division 1	Division 2	Division 3	Division 4
Gross sales	845,960	610,405	932,008	710,503
Direct costs	491,315	407,211	539,914	412,088
Gross profit	354,645	203,194	392,094	298,415
Expenses	303,900	219,816	336,196	255,598
Net profit	50,745	(13,622)	55,898	42,817

Allocation with three divisions

	Division 1	Division 2	Division 3	Division 4
Gross sales	845,960	0	932,008	710,503
Direct costs	491,315	0	539,914	412,088
Gross profit	354,645	0	392,094	298,415
Expenses	341,873	0	372,039	291,598
Net profit	12,772	0	20,055	6,817

With the closing of one division, net profits would have been reduced from $135,838 to only $39,644. This example reveals the problem of cost allocation. A division that appears to be losing money on a purely allocation basis actually absorbs a portion of overhead that will not go away—it is fixed. And some forms of nonfixed overhead will continue to a degree, even if the division is closed. The effect on the other divisions and on the company as a whole proves that a company may be better off living with a divisional loss.

Figure 4-3 shows why this is true. Using an arbitrary example of $150,000 in total fixed overhead, four divisions will each absorb one-fourth, on average. But with only three divisions, each must now absorb one-third. One division may appear to be losing money when, in fact, it carries a considerable share of overhead—enough to make it profitable—and that overhead will not go away just because the division is closed.

USING ALLOCATION TECHNIQUES

Understanding the methods used by accountants to break down costs and expenses can help you to better control and budget work in your own department. The techniques of allocation can be applied to your own budget, to ongoing projects, and to the control and scheduling of employee time.

Example: You are preparing a budget for your department for the coming year. Your plans include the addition of two new employees, and you know you will be expected to develop three major projects.

Figure 4-3.
Fixed overhead allocations.

	FOUR DIVISIONS	THREE DIVISIONS
	$150,000 total	$150,000 total
DIVISION 1	$37,500	$50,000
DIVISION 2	37,500	50,000
DIVISION 3	37,500	50,000
DIVISION 4	37,500	

By developing expense estimates on an allocated basis, you will be able to:

1. Support and prove your budgeted assumptions
2. Track expenses throughout the year
3. Plan the timing of expenses

Example: Your department is developing a midyear budget plan for a long-term project. In estimating overall costs, you run into difficulties. But by breaking the project down into segments, you are able to more closely estimate time and expenses for each phase.

Example: Some employees in your department have a heavy workload while others are often idle. To better distribute work, you develop a system for allocation. Those with heavier workloads are asked to break up their assignments and share them with others. A comparison of estimated hours required for each task, with the available hours, makes your allocation system a workable one.

Allocation is a valuable technique if used in a proper manner. In order to develop the best possible allocation procedure, especially for nonfinancial tasks, follow these steps:

1. Develop the means for allocation based on the attributes of a task. For example, the allocation of employee time to workload should be done on the basis of hours; project budgets should be done on a combination of material/labor cost and time needed for each phase.

2. Apply the assumed allocation method to the task and then review results. Does it appear to be reasonable, based on your experience? If not, return to the first step and reevaluate your assumptions.

3. Track the allocation. Is it working? If not, find out why. Perhaps your assumptions were flawed, or other factors not considered at first have entered the picture. Tracking is not limited to finding out what isn't working; it also provides you with the means for direct management, control, and budgeting of task phases.

If you develop a departmental budget each year, you will find allocation a useful technique for supporting assumptions. A well-structured budget is difficult to change. The documented use of allocations helps you to defend your budget and keep it intact.

Example: You are working on the new budget for your department. In the past, you had problems with budgets for office supplies and entertainment. Your budget last year consisted of percentage increases over the previous year's levels. Thus, variances were impossible to explain and responsibility for the problem could not be identified, and steps could not be taken to fix the problem.

This year, you decide to allocate expenses by employee. For office supplies, you determine a reasonable level for use of each of the eleven employees in your department and then add bulk purchase expenses (for letterhead and file folders, for example), based on previous use levels. You document all of your assumptions on a per-employee basis.

You use a similar approach to budget entertainment expenses. Each employee is assigned a specific monthly entertainment budget based on activity levels and customer or vendor contact. You make it clear to all employees that they will be responsible for all variances; if they go over their budget one month, they will be expected to absorb it during the following month.

Be sure your per-employee allocations are reasonable and fair. They must be able to control expense levels directly in order for this procedure to work. It's the same argument against accounting departments charging you for rent and utilities. For allocations to work, they must be fair and controllable on the receiving end.

Allocation for departmental budgets makes variance analysis practical and specific. It also provides a controllable budget that, if monitored each month, will enable you to control expenses in your department. By using allocation techniques, you solve the problems experienced in the past and bring expenses under control.

The next chapter shows how information is gathered and processed by accountants and how those techniques will help you reduce the time required for information retrieval. You will see how documentation techniques can help you respond to requests, answer questions, and back up your claims with facts.

Chapter 5

The Information Puzzle

Every report, financial statement, record, and worksheet the accountant prepares is based on written proof or on another document that shows how estimates were developed. Verification is essential to the accountant. So complete is the dedication to proof in the accounting profession that, to others, it often seems that the numbers matter to accountants more than the facts behind them. In truth, attention to detail is a primary reason that top management often depends so much on accountants and completely respects their financial information. Their reports are built on documented fact or the interpretation of facts.

You, too, can develop the discipline to verify what you claim and can be prepared to prove what you report. It's simply a matter of approaching problems with an eye to the source of your information.

THE AUDIT TRAIL

One of the most important fundamental ideas behind accounting is that every number written on a statement or in the books must be traced back to a source document. For example, each entry in the general ledger expense accounts must be supported by an invoice, statement, receipt, or other voucher. If no voucher is available, a worksheet, memo, or other document must be placed in the files to explain the entry. Proof may also consist of a contractual obligation. For example, payments of rent are documented by the signed rental agreement; salary payments are verified by an employment agreement.

This *audit trail*, as it's called, is applied not only to the information in the books. It also comes into play in the methods accountants use to argue a point, to support a claim, and to influence decisions. You can make use of the principles of audit trail to improve your influence in the decision-making process.

Think of the audit trail as a four-level process (summarized in Figure 5-1):

1. Source documents. Source documents comprise the first level in the process. These include all vouchers, receipts, and other papers that prove a transaction occurred, tell how much money was exchanged, and indicate the business nature of the transaction.

Source documents are always the starting point for the accounting entry. And you can apply the same standard, even to the nonaccounting reports you prepare. Each fact you present should be supported with the equivalent of a source—if not a document, then at least a verifiable information source.

2. Books of original entry. The second level in the accounting process is called the books of original entry, where source documents are recorded and arranged in a consistent, logical format. Accountants code transactions from source documents and record them in journals, with coding for eventual posting to the general ledger.

You can create your own version of "books of original entry" by organizing and arranging your research to help finalize a report. You need not formalize your department to the degree that the accounting department does. But you can use the methodical system to prepare and cross-reference your reports so that you will later be able to trace information back to its origin.

3. Books of final entry. Accountants put transactions into proper classifications at the third level. They record information from journals into the general ledger.

Figure 5-1.
The audit trail.

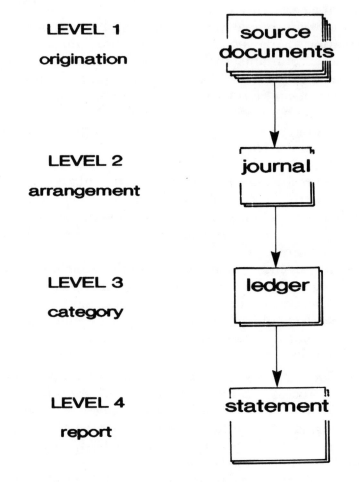

LEVEL 1
origination

source documents

LEVEL 2
arrangement

journal

LEVEL 3
category

ledger

LEVEL 4
report

statement

The nonaccountant's version of books of final entry is the preliminary draft of a report. Once your source documents have been organized and arranged, you're ready to summarize them logically.

4. Statements. The fourth level is the financial statement. This is the accountant's report, built on the preceding three levels. Every number on the statement can be traced back to the other three levels and verified beyond any doubt.

Imagine how much confidence you will have in your reports with the same level of verification at your fingertips. You can use the four-level audit trail to improve your reporting capability, as well as your reputation as a manager who can promptly prove everything stated in the report, whether financial or nonfinancial.

The value in this methodical recording and reporting process is in the fact that information is verified all along the way. Nothing goes into the financial statement that has not already been subjected to strict accounting standards of audit trail. Even when some information must be estimated, it is done through worksheets for documentation.

Example: The accounting department is preparing financial statements for the end of the quarter. During the last month, the company sponsored a national convention and spent thousands of dollars in travel and related convention expenses. But as of the closing of the books, none of the receipts or invoices has been received. The accountant estimates the expense for each category and prepares a worksheet. The entry is put into the books as an accrual, so that financial statements will show the expense as accurately as possible.

By applying this same routine in developing your reports and in building your arguments, you will gain the reputation as a thorough, concise manager. Your information will be dependable, traceable, and complete.

THE AUDIT TRAIL AND CREDIBILITY

When managers present information in meetings and are questioned, or when their conclusions are challenged, they often have difficulty responding, because they have not built in their own audit trail. The methodical and complete verification processes that accountants practice in everything they do are not common to all managers, although they can and should be. Learning to apply this level of discipline to your daily reporting and communicating tasks will greatly improve your credibility and effectiveness in the organization.

Example: During a management meeting, two individuals are asked for reports. The accountant presents a balance sheet and income statement, and the marketing manager presents a revised income forecast for the second half.

The accountant is questioned at length. The vice-president wants to know why office supply expenses are high for the current quarter and why net profits are below budget. The reported depreciation estimate and interest expense figures are also challenged. In each case, the accountant is able to give an explanation of fact or estimate. All questions are resolved by proof found in ledgers or journals or on worksheets.

The marketing manager then makes his report. He claims income will be up during the third and fourth quarters, and the vice-president asks how that will be achieved. The marketing manager cannot verify his estimates with worksheets to prove the point or point to a trend that supports his claim. The result: The higher sales the marketing manager predicts are doubted.

The difference between these two cases is that the accountant came to the meeting with solid proof in hand. The sales estimates the marketing manager presented may be just as correct, but there was no proof. So the credibility of the accountant's report is much greater than that of the marketing manager.

BUILDING VERIFICATION LINKS

Once you're prepared to prove everything you claim in a report, you will save yourself time. You will not need to go back over your own work, search through files, or build an audit trail in response to questions from others, because it will already be in your hands.

Think of the process as a series of verification links. The techniques of audit trail are a way of building an information base or system, not just for a solitary report, but as a revised approach to all of the issues you face in your management task. Set the standard that every report you prepare must contain facts that can be tied to a source. You have many resources for the development of these links, and you may use them in all of the communications you practice.

Four of the most commonly used verification links are:

1. Financial records. Many reports, including those prepared outside of the accounting department, are based on financial information, including budgets, financial statements, and records you keep in your department.

2. Historical information. Your company's published statements, the history of workload in your department, the development of employee resources, and the markets and competition your company deals with are all examples of historical information, which is both financial and nonfinancial.

3. Analysis. Many of the opinions managers develop and many of the decisions made each day are based on analysis. You define a problem by analyzing its attributes and then interpreting the significance of those attributes to arrive at a solution. You may depend on analysis provided by employees, by other managers, or from sources outside of the company.

4. Research. The fourth common verification link, research, may consist of consultation with other departments, with employees, or with top management. You might develop the means for analysis by reading reports that others prepare.

When the verification links available to you are used to create an information bank, you support your claims and conclusions. This support helps you to strengthen your arguments and draw conclusions more decisively and assertively than if you must depend on estimates and hunches that have not been verified. Figure 5-2 shows the connection between reports and verification links.

Figure 5-2.
Verification links.

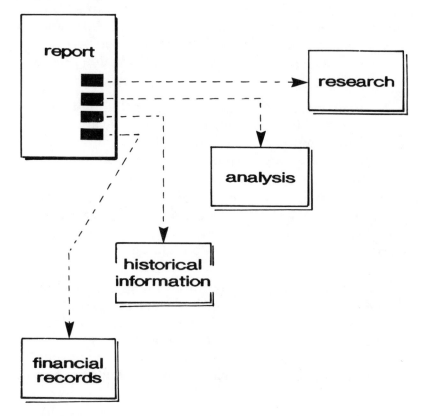

ESTABLISHING AN AUDIT STANDARD

You can never make your point by simply presenting your case and expecting a positive response. Be prepared to present a series of facts proving your point. To verify that your point is correct and complete, always refer to the four basic information sources: financial information, historical information, analysis, and research.

Don't overlook the accounting department as an excellent source of financial information. Their task is to gather and arrange information, and those records can be most helpful in making arguments based on the numbers. This information is available not only for departmental or companywide transactions, but also for budgets and forecasts for this year or previous years.

Current information is useful but very limited. It does very little to estimate the future, and most of your arguments must look forward. One way to support arguments with facts is to depend on consistent trends found in historical information.

Anticipate growth in the near future by analyzing related transactions for the most recent past. A short-term analysis is very dependable; but the longer the time you're looking ahead, the less value an estimate will have.

Report facts about how other departments have dealt with problems similar to yours, including the outcome. This research is useful not only to show where success has been achieved, but also to isolate past solution attempts that failed. How does your idea improve on previous attempts? How will you avoid similar problems? Internal research is valuable because all managers can learn from past mistakes, but all too often, the case histories within the company are ignored or overlooked.

Any report you give should be as brief as possible. Your main points should be summarized on the first page, ending with a very specific conclusion that solves the stated problem. Then make the request for approval based on your conclusions. Be specific. If presented as a profitable solution, how can management say no?

A problem most managers eventually face is having to make their case when their argument goes against the accounting department's recommendation. It suggests a hiring freeze, but you need one more employee; it argues against a new telephone system, but you know it would save thousands of dollars every year; or it disapproves an idea because there's no budget for it, while you would like to see the company take advantage of a marketing opportunity.

All of these issues can be resolved by using the techniques of audit trail and verification. As any lawyer knows, you win cases by presenting evidence. And you lose cases when you're not prepared. The same is true in business. Accountants have a tremendous advantage in the fact that their report, the financial statement, is verified and documented. This format is dictated by acceptable practice so that a well-prepared format is expected from the accounting department.

You can be perceived as well prepared by applying the same techniques and principles that accountants use every day. Once you begin thinking in terms of verification, the process becomes natural and obvious. You will automatically depend on verified information, learn to link facts to conclusions to support opinions with certainties, and anticipate questions with exceptionally well-prepared information.

Information is best used in two ways. First, as we discussed above, is the documentation of facts in a report. You will win your point when you're able to prove the facts you claim. The second use of information is to set standards to monitor results in the department.

Example: Your department is beginning work on a very complex long-term project. It will require many hours to complete, and you have a deadline four months away. You also must establish a budget for the project. So you develop a series of phases, treating each one as a smaller project on its own, including deadlines, scheduling, and budgets for each segment.

In order to track progress, you create a monitoring system that uses audit verification techniques. You follow the schedule used by your employees, and you watch your budget, including weekly and monthly reviews. Whenever you fall behind schedule, and whenever you exceed a segment's budget, you take immediate action.

To achieve this level of control, you should use a well-documented standard (schedule and budget) to begin with. Otherwise, how will you know when you're succeeding? Once you have set up your standards and they are well understood by everyone involved, staying on schedule is a matter of supervisory control. A simplified version of the audit trail approach to scheduling and budgeting is shown in Figure 5-3.

Figure 5-3.
Establishing audit standards.

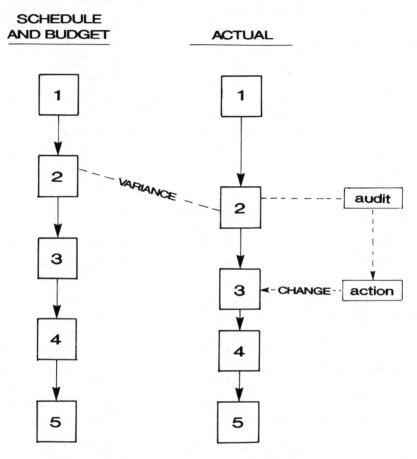

In Figure 5-3, the schedule or the budget (or both) show a variance during the second phase. Your response is to audit the conditions and identify the cause of the variance and to then take action to get your department back to your standard. If it's a budgeting problem, you might discover that the original budget was flawed or that too much money was spent during that phase. Corrective action may involve better controls, a change in the approval procedures, or closer review and supervision of work. If it's a scheduling problem, the timing of subsequent phases must be accelerated so that the final deadline can still be met. So a variance leads to an audit (investigation), then to action and change. That's how audit trail helps you to stay in control.

This procedure is identical to the investigative functions used by accountants and auditors as applied to financial records. The same methodical approach works equally well in management and control situations. Chances are, you're already applying this technique to a degree in your daily routine, without clearly defining it as a methodical and precise approach. By defining the process well and by thinking in terms of audit trail as a constant form of monitoring you will ensure successful and timely completion of a task.

AUDITING AND QUALITY CONTROL

Audit trail techniques add validation to the volume of paperwork that flows through every organization. By applying these techniques, you will increase your influence, win well-conceived arguments, and upgrade the problem-solving challenges you face every day. Audit trail also ensures higher quality in the work you produce.

Most people hear the word *audit* and picture internal or external auditors going over the books in detail, testing transactions and adjusting financial statements. You can apply auditing in your own department in a somewhat less detailed manner, to test for and improve accuracy and quality.

Example: Employees in your department submit check requests, which must be coded to the proper general ledger accounts. You review and approve these requests each day. You will improve accuracy and eliminate coding errors by checking all coding, in addition to examining the nature and amount of the request.

Example: Your department prepares a status report at the end of each month and submits it to the accounting department, from which a budget report is prepared. With a short deadline, the status report is always prepared under pressure. You know that errors have been made in the past. So you institute a final accuracy test as part of the procedure. It takes only a few minutes, but it eliminates math and spelling errors.

Example: One of the employees in your department is chronically inaccurate in math. You do not always check his work, but you can delegate responsibility to an assistant. You meet with the employee and instruct him to double-check his own work, find and correct obvious math errors before finalizing a report, and then submit the report to your assistant for a final check.

In each of these cases, a concern for quality and accuracy drives the auditing steps you take. You may equate this form of quality control with the steps taken in a factory to reduce the number of product defects. In a manufacturing environment, the problem and its solutions are certainly tangible and can be monitored very specifically. A particular shift with a higher than average frequency of defects is quickly identified and the problem is isolated. But for the administrative manager, dealing with reports, memos, and other forms of communication, quality is more elusive and less tangible. Thus, it may seem more difficult to control.

Quality can be controlled, regardless of how intangible your "product." The solution is to first establish very specific standards for your department. Next, set up simple but effective controls (direct review, delegated review, and instructions to employees to double-check their own work, for example). Finally, monitor your control procedures through a periodic audit (review).

These steps ensure that your standards will be respected, enforced, and met. As long as you are willing and able to follow through on the rules you establish for your department, you will make the best use of auditing techniques. It is not practical or possible to check every piece of paper that leaves your department. The best way to ensure that your standards are met is to use audit trail techniques through delegating and periodic monitoring.

CONFIDENCE IN YOUR NUMBERS

Putting audit trail techniques to work in a nonaccounting department will help you in all forms of communication in your company. Stepping into the ring with an accounting heavyweight might seem intimidating, especially if you are uncomfortable with financial reporting or if you suffer from math phobia. To offset this problem, keep these points in mind:

1. You are an expert. You do particular things well. Just as accountants are comfortable with numbers, you are comfortable with a range of skills and tasks. You deal with issues of direct concern to you and your employees, which you know and understand better than anyone else. In that respect, you're not in competition with the accountant, even when you communicate in financial terms. Your own expertise is worth much more than the simple ability to work with numbers.

2. Facts cannot be disputed. As long as your points are supported with complete and relevant facts, you have no reason to fear debate. Once other managers understand that you are willing and able to support your position with verified information, you will gain a greater degree of influence.

3. There is no great technique secret. Accountants use commonsense procedures to verify their information. You have a distinct advantage. To the accountant, the numbers are the product. But to you, the numbers are a tool used to explain the product or service you offer.

4. Confidence grows from knowledge. If you are uncertain about how to win your point or how to express your ideas in financial terms, be willing to research, ask questions, and seek help, even from your company's accounting department.

5. The accountant is not an adversary. If you make the effort to create an ally of your accountant, your task will be much easier. The response from the accounting department to a professional approach to problem solving will probably be positive and cooperative.

6. Positive expression leads to results. You are most effective when you express what you want rather than what you don't want. State your ideas in positive terms. For example, ask for permission to hire a new employee so that you can help improve the company's profits, rather than complaining about overtime and too much work.

You do not need to master all of the skills that accountants use. Rather, you need only to master the relatively simple techniques for proving what's expressed in financial terms. That means building an audit trail whenever you state a fact or opinion, and it means adding a methodical approach to the processes you complete. If you evaluate the significance of this idea, you'll conclude that it is all common sense, and nothing more. You probably already perform many of your duties with a well-conceived approach. But some managers fail to take the technique far enough. Perhaps you're very thorough in developing and proving facts in order to prepare a report, but you then leave your proof in your office when you go to a meeting. Or you might be very clear when setting goals with employees in your department, but when preparing a staffing budget, you don't develop, expand, and prove your assumptions.

Think of audit trail as a technique you can apply to every aspect of your job, including communication with others. Don't go to a meeting without your worksheets. Take your proof with you. A well-researched report is of little value unless you anticipate a challenge and you can answer with solid facts.

Chapter 6 deals with the problem of math phobia by tackling the fundamentals of time value of money. Even if you are not directly involved with figuring out the compound growth of money, knowing how time value of money works will improve your ability to communicate. And the day will come when you will need to know how to figure out the present or future value of money. Accountants and top management understand this form of communication and so can you.

Chapter 6

The Time Value of Money

Financial people, in their need to keep score of corporate activities, communicate with numbers, which they describe and qualify in terms of yield, profit, and return. An investment earns a given yield over a period of time, profits represent a percentage of sales for one year, and the cost of borrowing money is translated to a percentage of the amount borrowed.

Confusion is created by the fact that such terms as yield, profit, and return may mean different things in different situations. Yet, the same descriptive wording might be used in unlike situations.

Example: Profit for the year could mean the *gross* profit (before expenses are deducted), the *operating* profit (before accounting for interest income and expense, capital gains, and other nonoperating items), the *pretax* profit, or the *after-tax* profit, which is the final bottom line after taxes.

Example: Yield on an investment could mean the *nominal* or stated rate (9 percent per year), the *current* yield based on a purchase at discount or premium, or the *compounded* rate (9.38 percent on a stated yield of 9 percent when compounding occurs monthly, for instance). With all of the terminology in use, the typical nonaccounting manager is confused and uncertain when confronted with a yield, profit, or return.

COMPOUNDING INTEREST

The methods of calculating percentages of return vary by compounding period. Compounding may occur based on a number of different methods:

1. *Daily* compounding is used by banks for paying interest. An annual rate is divided by the days in the year (this may be done on the basis of a 365-day year or a 360-day year). The result is the daily rate.
2. *Monthly* compounding is used for loan payments, including mortgages. The annual rate is divided by 12, and the result is the monthly rate of interest.
3. *Quarterly* compounding is figured by dividing the annual rate by four, and then multiplying a principal amount by the quarterly rate, four times per year.
4. *Semiannual* compounding involves two periods per year, with one-half of the annual rate applied to each period.
5. *Annual* compounding occurs at the stated rate. For example, to compound at 9 percent annually, the principal amount is multiplied by 9 percent, and the new balance is carried forward to the next year.

In comparison to compounding, *simple* interest does not accumulate. With compounding, an account earns interest on interest, so that yield over time not only increases, it accelerates. For example, annual compounding at 9 percent involves an ever-growing balance:

Year	Interest	Balance
		$100.00
1	$ 9.00	109.00
2	9.81	118.81
3	10.69	129.50

In comparison, simple interest does not increase the principal but involves the same amount of interest each period:

Year	Interest	Balance
		$100.00
1	$ 9.00	109.00
2	9.00	118.00
3	9.00	127.00

Most business applications call for compounding on a monthly or quarterly basis. In a one-year period, the difference in interest paid under one method or the other is not great. However, over several years, varying compounding methods make ever-increasing differences.

Whenever you communicate in terms of a percentage of interest, be sure to specify how that interest has been computed. When the choice is left to you to use one method over another, follow these guidelines:

1. When expressing a rate of return on money left on deposit or invested, use an annual interest rate, unless you are comparing a yield to an alternative in which interest is earned on some other basis.
2. When describing yield on capital, use a rate that corresponds to the method used in financial statements. This yield may be quarterly or annual, depending on the method employed by the accounting department. Annual yield is the usual method used.

Figure 6-1 illustrates compound interest for one year computed on a monthly and a quarterly basis.

For nonaccounting managers, knowing how to calculate interest can be useful in several ways:

1. Preparing a departmental budget in which assumed monthly or quarterly inflation factors are to be used. For example, budget items often are increased by a percentage over the prior month's budget, which is a form of monthly compounding.
2. Estimating the cost of borrowing money when a rec-

ommendation you include in a report would require debt financing. As long as a lender would require monthly repayments, chances are that interest will be calculated based on each month's outstanding balance. Thus, monthly compounding would apply.
3. Calculating the after-interest benefits to the company of a proposal you are making that will save money. Use annual compounding, to correspond to the method used for financial statement reporting.

Figure 6-1.
Compound interest, monthly and quarterly.

| MONTH | 9% INTEREST | |
	MONTHLY	QUARTERLY
	100.00	100.00
Jan	100.75	
Feb	101.51	
Mar	102.27	102.25
Apr	103.03	
May	103.81	
Jun	104.59	104.55
Jul	105.37	
Aug	106.16	
Sep	106.96	106.90
Oct	107.76	
Nov	108.57	
Dec	109.38	109.31
	9.38%	**9.31%**

Whenever interest is compounded more frequently than once per year, the calculation of periodic interest is done by first figuring out the periodic rate. The annual rate must be divided by the number of compound periods per year—twelve for monthly, four for quarterly, and so forth. To determine actual interest, add 1 to the periodic rate and use the sum as the compound multiplier.

Example: At 9 percent, the monthly rate is .0075:

$$\frac{9\%}{12} = .0075$$

The steps required to compute the periodic rate and compound multipliers are summarized in Figure 6-2.

The more compound periods in a year, the more steps are involved in figuring interest over a period of years. Monthly compounding requires twelve computations per year; quarterly compounding calls for only four. This consideration becomes important when the yield is figured over a number of years. For this reason, compound interest tables are very necessary shortcuts for determining the time value of money.

COMPOUND INTEREST TABLES

There are six different compound interest tables, each for a distinct and different calculation of the time value of money. Books containing tables for a range of interest rates and compounding methods can be purchased in most bookstores.

Even among experienced accounting and financial experts, there is considerable confusion about the proper uses of each compound interest table. But by reading about each one in a context that applies to you in your daily management task, and then by seeing how each table is constructed, you will discover that making tables simple to use is not difficult.

The tables are set up to report values "per 1 dollar," so

Figure 6-2.
Periodic rate.

STEP 1

convert annual rate from
percentage to decimal form:

9%	=	.09

STEP 2

divide by the number of
periods in one year

monthly $\dfrac{.09}{12}$ = .0075

quarterly $\dfrac{.09}{4}$ = .0225

semiannually $\dfrac{.09}{2}$ = .0450

STEP 3

add 1 to arrive at the
compound multiplier

monthly	=	1.0075
quarterly	=	1.0225
semiannually	=	1.0450

that a single factor is given at each interest rate and for each
time period. So when you have a factor of 1, you must multiply an amount of money by that factor.

Every table reports the following information:

1. Compounding method and rate
2. Type of table
3. Time, in months and/or years
4. Factors

Factors (values per one dollar) usually are carried out a number of decimal places. For the purpose of illustration, we show factors to six decimal places. By identifying the correct table, rate, and compounding method, you need only to find the applicable time period and factor. You then multiply the amount by that factor.

Accumulated Value of 1

The accumulated value of 1—also called the future value of 1—is the future value of a single deposit of money at a given rate of interest after a specified number of years. Figure 6-3 shows a sample page from a book of compound interest tables for the accumulated value of 1.

Example: Your company deposits $10,000 in a mutual fund account that is estimated to yield 9 percent per year, compounded monthly. You want to know what that deposit will be worth in ten years. By referring to a compound interest table for the accumulated value of 1, at 9 percent compounded monthly, you will find a factor of 2.451357. If you multiply the $10,000 deposit by that factor, you will arrive at the ten-year value:

$$\$10,000 \times 2.451357 = \$24,513.57$$

Example: You deposit $100 in a money market account on January 1. Interest is calculated and added at the rate of 9 percent, compounded monthly. What will the account be worth in one year? The twelve-month factor is 1.093807:

$$\$100.00 \times 1.093807 = \$109.38$$

To prove the calculation, you could compute each month's interest, as shown in Figure 6-1. That involves multiplying the original deposit by the compound multiplier (at 9 percent, that's 1.0075), for each of the twelve months. Most hand-held calculators enable you to do this calculation easily, with the following steps:

Figure 6-3.
Sample interest tables for accumulated value of 1.

			MONTHLY
Accumulated Value of 1			
months	*8.50%*	*9.00%*	*9.50%*
1	1.007083	1.007500	1.007917
2	1.014217	1.015056	1.015896
3	1.021401	1.022669	1.023939
4	1.028636	1.030339	1.032045
5	1.035922	1.038067	1.040215
6	1.043260	1.045852	1.048450
7	1.050650	1.053696	1.056750
8	1.058092	1.061599	1.065116
9	1.065586	1.069561	1.073548
10	1.073134	1.077583	1.082047
11	1.080736	1.085664	1.090614
years			
1	1.088391	1.093807	1.099248
2	1.184595	1.196414	1.208345
3	1.289302	1.308645	1.328271
4	1.403265	1.431405	1.460098
5	1.527301	1.565681	1.605009
6	1.662300	1.712553	1.764303
7	1.809232	1.873202	1.939406
8	1.969152	2.048921	2.131887
9	2.143207	2.241124	2.343472
10	2.332647	2.451357	2.576055
11	2.538832	2.681311	2.831723
12	2.763242	2.932837	3.112764
13	3.007487	3.207957	3.421699
14	3.273321	3.508886	3.761294
15	3.562653	3.838043	4.134593
16	3.877559	4.198078	4.544942
17	4.220300	4.591887	4.996016
18	4.593337	5.022638	5.491859
19	4.999346	5.493796	6.036912
20	5.441243	6.009152	6.636061

1. Enter 1.0075 (compound multiplier)   1.0075
2. Depress × (multiply)   ×
3. Enter 100.00 (deposit amount)   100.00
4. Depress = (total)   =
5. Depress = eleven more times   =

Once you know how to calculate the compound multiplier for a rate of interest, you can build your own tables. At 9 percent, the compound multiplier for monthly calculations is 1.0075. The steps required to build a table for the accumulated value of 1 are shown in Figure 6-4.

Accumulated Value of 1 Per Period

The second table shows the future value of a series of deposits at a given rate of interest and for a specified period of time. Figure 6-5 shows a page from a book of compound interest tables for the accumulated value of 1 per period.

Example: Your company deposits $1,000 per month in an account that will yield 9 percent interest, compounded monthly. What will that account be worth after five years? The answer is found by checking the table for the accumulated value of 1 per period. The five-year factor is 75.424137. Multiply the amount of each month's deposit by this factor to find the five-year value:

$$\$1,000 \times 75.424137 = \$75,424.14$$

Example: You ask your employer to withhold $100 per month from your paycheck and transfer it to an account that pays 9 percent, compounded monthly. You want to know what your account will be worth after one year. By checking a table for the accumulated value of 1 per period, at 9 percent interest compounded monthly, the factor is 12.507586:

$$\$100.00 \times 12.507586 = \$1,250.76$$

Calculating this by hand is more involved than the steps for a single deposit because deposits are made at the begin-

Figure 6-4.
Accumulated value of 1.

	9% FACTOR

STEP 1

    1st month = compound multiplier   1.007500

STEP 2

    subsequent months: multiply the previous factor by the compound multiplier

        2nd month:

            1.007500 × 1.0075 =   1.015056

        3rd month:

            1.015056 × 1.0075 =   1.022669

TABLE 9% MONTHLY	
month	factor
1	1.007500
2	1.015056
3	1.022669
4	1.030339
5	1.038067
6	1.045852

ning of each month, rather than in a single sum. Because interest is calculated at the end of each month, the value after one month is always equal to 1. To figure subsequent periods, multiply the previous factor by the compound multiplier and add 1. For example, the first month's value of a $100 deposit per month will be $100. At the end of the second month, the account will be worth $200.75:

Figure 6-5.
Sample interest tables for accumulated value of 1 per period.

			MONTHLY
Accumulated Value of 1 per period			
months	*8.50%*	*9.00%*	*9.50%*
1	1.000000	1.000000	1.000000
2	2.007083	2.007500	2.007917
3	3.021300	3.022556	3.023813
4	4.042701	4.045225	4.047751
5	5.071337	5.075565	5.079796
6	6.107259	6.113631	6.120011
7	7.150519	7.159484	7.168461
8	8.201168	8.213180	8.225211
9	9.259260	9.274779	9.290328
10	10.324846	10.344339	10.363876
11	11.397980	11.421922	11.445923
years			
1	12.478716	12.507586	12.536537
2	26.060437	26.188471	26.317295
3	40.842659	41.152716	41.465760
4	56.931495	57.520711	58.117673
5	74.442437	75.424137	76.422249
6	93.501188	95.007028	96.543509
7	114.244559	116.426928	118.661756
8	136.821455	139.856164	142.975186
9	161.393943	165.483223	169.701665
10	188.138416	193.514277	199.080682
11	217.246858	224.174837	231.375495
12	248.928220	257.711570	266.875491
13	283.409927	294.394279	305.898776
14	320.939504	334.518079	348.795027
15	361.786353	378.405769	395.948628
16	406.243693	426.410427	447.782110
17	454.630657	478.918252	504.759939
18	507.294589	536.351674	567.392681
19	564.613533	599.172747	636.241570
20	626.998951	667.886870	711.923546

Previous factor × compound multiplier
$$1.000000 \times 1.007500 = 1.007500$$
Add 1
$$1.007500 + 1 \qquad = 2.00750$$

This step is repeated for the number of periods in question. The steps are summarized in Figure 6-6.

A table can be constructed using a hand calculator by following these steps:

1. Enter the previous factor
   (third month calculation)   2.007500
2. Depress × (multiply)   ×
3. Enter compound multiplier   1.0075
4. Add 1   + 1
5. Enter = (total), to arrive   =
   at the third month factor   3.022556

Present Value of 1

The previous sections described the future value of money. A deposit or a series of deposits grows at a compound rate to its future value. The opposite of these calculations is present value.

The present value of 1 is the amount required today to accumulate one dollar in the future, given a rate of interest, a compounding method, and a period of time. Figure 6-7 shows a sample page from a book of compound interest tables for the present value of 1.

Example: Your company needs to accumulate a fund worth $10,000 in five years, in order to retire a debt in a single payment. How much must be left on deposit today, assuming 9 percent interest, compounded monthly, in a single deposit? By checking the table for the present value of 1, the factor for five years is 0.638700. The required deposit of $10,000 is multiplied by this factor:

$$\$10,000 \times 0.638700 = \$6,387.00$$

(continued on page 88)

Figure 6-6.
Accumulated value of 1 per period.

	9% FACTOR

STEP 1

   1st month = 1   1.000000

STEP 2

   subsequent months: multiply the
previous factor by the compound
multiplier and add 1

      2nd month:

         1.000000 x 1.0075

         plus 1   =   2.007500

      3rd month:

         2.007500 x 1.0075

         plus 1   =   3.022556

TABLE 9% MONTHLY	
month	factor
1	1.000000
2	2.007500
3	3.022556
4	4.045225
5	5.075565
6	6.113631

Figure 6-7.
Sample interest tables for present value of 1.

			MONTHLY
Present Value of 1			
months	*8.50%*	*9.00%*	*9.50%*
1	0.992966	0.992556	0.992146
2	0.985982	0.985167	0.984353
3	0.979048	0.977833	0.976621
4	0.972161	0.970554	0.968950
5	0.965324	0.963329	0.961340
6	0.958534	0.956158	0.953789
7	0.951792	0.949040	0.946297
8	0.945098	0.941975	0.938865
9	0.938450	0.934963	0.931490
10	0.931850	0.928003	0.924174
11	0.925296	0.921095	0.916915
years			
1	0.918788	0.914238	0.909713
2	0.844171	0.835831	0.827578
3	0.775613	0.764149	0.752859
4	0.712624	0.698614	0.684885
5	0.654750	0.638700	0.623049
6	0.601576	0.583924	0.566796
7	0.552721	0.533845	0.515622
8	0.507833	0.488062	0.469068
9	0.466590	0.446205	0.426717
10	0.428698	0.407937	0.388190
11	0.393882	0.372952	0.353142
12	0.361894	0.340967	0.321258
13	0.332504	0.311725	0.292253
14	0.305500	0.284991	0.265866
15	0.280690	0.260549	0.241862
16	0.257894	0.238204	0.220025
17	0.236950	0.217775	0.200159
18	0.217707	0.199099	0.182088
19	0.200026	0.182024	0.165648
20	0.183782	0.166413	0.150692

If that amount is placed on deposit today, it will grow to $10,000 in five years, at 9 percent interest compounded monthly.

Example: You want to accumulate $1,200 in your mutual fund account in one year. If you will earn 9 percent, compounded monthly, how much must you deposit today? Checking the present value of 1 table, the 12-month factor is 0.914238:

$$\$1,200 \times 0.914238 = \$1,097.09$$

If you deposit that amount today, it will be worth $1,200 in one year, at 9 percent interest compounded monthly.

You will recall that to calculate the accumulated value of 1, you needed to know the periodic compound multiplier for a rate of interest. At 9 percent compounded monthly, that multiplier is 1.007500. To build a present value of 1 table, you also need to use the compound multiplier. However, because present value is the opposite of accumulated value, the calculation is different.

Divide 1 by the compound multiplier to arrive at the first month's factor. For subsequent months, divide the previous factor by the compound multiplier. The steps to building this table are shown in Figure 6-8.

This calculation can be performed on a hand calculator by following these steps:

1. Enter 1 or the previous factor	1
2. Depress ÷ (divide)	÷
3. Enter the compound multiplier	1.0075
4. Depress = (total) to compute the factor	= 0.992556

Sinking Fund Factors

A sinking fund describes a series of payments required to accumulate a specified amount in the future. A sinking fund factors table provides the factors for amounts that must be

Figure 6-8.
Present value of 1.

		9% FACTOR
STEP 1		
divide 1 by the compound multiplier		
$\frac{1}{1.0075}$	=	0.992556
STEP 2		
divide the previous factor by the compound multiplier		
2nd month: $\frac{0.992556}{1.0075}$	=	0.985167
3rd month: $\frac{0.985167}{1.0075}$	=	0.977833

TABLE 9% MONTHLY	
month	factor
1	0.992556
2	0.985167
3	0.977833
4	0.970554
5	0.963329
6	0.956158

deposited periodically to save one dollar in the future. Figure 6-9 shows a sample page from a book of compound interest payments for sinking fund factors.

Example: Your company wants to build a fund worth $10,000 over the next five years. It is assumed that savings will earn 9 percent compounded monthly. How much must be deposited at the beginning of each month to build this fund? Referring to a sinking fund factors table, the factor is 0.013258. Multiply the target amount of $10,000 by this factor:

$$\$10,000 \times 0.013258 = \$132.58$$

Example: You want to build a savings account of $1,200 in one year. Assuming you can earn 9 percent with monthly compounding, how much must you deposit at the beginning of each month? The sinking fund table shows a factor for 12 months of 0.079951:

$$\$1,200 \times 0.079951 = \$95.94$$

To build a sinking fund factors table, divide 1 by the factor shown on the table for the accumulated value of 1 per period. This calculation is shown in Figure 6-10.

The first month is a factor of 1.000000. For the second month follow these steps on a hand calculator:

1. Enter 1	1
2. Depress ÷ (divide)	÷
3. Enter the factor from the table for accumulated value of 1 per period	2.007500
4. Depress = (total) to arrive at the sinking fund factor	0.498132

Present value of 1 Per Period

The fifth table is used to show how much must be deposited in a single sum to fund a series of future payments. Figure

Figure 6-9.
Sample interest tables for sinking fund factors.

			MONTHLY
Sinking Fund Factors			
months	*8.50%*	*9.00%*	*9.50%*
1	1.000000	1.000000	1.000000
2	0.498235	0.498132	0.498029
3	0.330983	0.330846	0.330708
4	0.247359	0.247205	0.247051
5	0.197187	0.197022	0.196858
6	0.163740	0.163569	0.163398
7	0.139850	0.139675	0.139500
8	0.121934	0.121756	0.121577
9	0.108000	0.107819	0.107639
10	0.096854	0.096671	0.096489
11	0.087735	0.087551	0.087367
years			
1	0.080136	0.079951	0.079767
2	0.038372	0.038185	0.037998
3	0.024484	0.024300	0.024116
4	0.017565	0.017385	0.017206
5	0.013433	0.013258	0.013085
6	0.010695	0.010526	0.010358
7	0.008753	0.008589	0.008427
8	0.007309	0.007150	0.006994
9	0.006196	0.006043	0.005893
10	0.005315	0.005168	0.005023
11	0.004603	0.004461	0.004322
12	0.004017	0.003880	0.003747
13	0.003528	0.003397	0.003269
14	0.003116	0.002989	0.002867
15	0.002764	0.002643	0.002526
16	0.002462	0.002345	0.002233
17	0.002200	0.002088	0.001981
18	0.001971	0.001864	0.001762
19	0.001771	0.001669	0.001572
20	0.001595	0.001497	0.001405

Figure 6-10.
Sinking fund factors.

9%
FACTOR

divide 1 by factors on the
table, accumulated value
of 1 per period:

1st month:

$$\frac{1}{1.000000} \quad = \quad 1.000000$$

2nd month:

$$\frac{1}{2.007500} \quad = \quad 0.498132$$

3rd month:

$$\frac{1}{3.022556} \quad = \quad 0.330846$$

TABLE 9% MONTHLY	
month	factor
1	1.000000
2	0.498132
3	0.330846
4	0.247205
5	0.197022
6	0.163569

6-11 shows a sample page from a book of compound interest
tables for the present value of 1 per period.

Example: Your company is required to pay $5,000 per month for
the next five months for the lease of equipment. Assuming 9 percent
interest compounded monthly, how much must be placed on deposit

Figure 6-11.
Sample interest tables for present value of 1 per period.

	MONTHLY		
	Present Value of 1 per Period		
months	*8.50%*	*9.00%*	*9.50%*
1	0.992966	0.992556	0.992146
2	1.978949	1.977723	1.976498
3	2.957996	2.955556	2.953119
4	3.930158	3.926110	3.922070
5	4.895482	4.889440	4.883409
6	5.854016	5.845598	5.837198
7	6.805808	6.794638	6.783496
8	7.750906	7.736613	7.722360
9	8.689356	8.671576	8.653851
10	9.621206	9.599580	9.578024
11	10.546501	10.520675	10.494940
years			
1	11.465289	11.434913	11.404653
2	21.999453	21.889146	21.779615
3	31.678112	31.446805	31.217856
4	40.570744	40.184782	39.803947
5	48.741183	48.173374	47.614827
6	56.248080	55.476849	54.720488
7	63.145324	62.153965	61.184601
8	69.482425	68.258439	67.065090
9	75.304875	73.839382	72.414648
10	80.654470	78.941693	77.281211
11	85.569611	83.606420	81.708388
12	90.085581	87.871092	85.735849
13	94.234798	91.770018	89.399684
14	98.047046	95.334564	92.732722
15	101.549693	98.593409	95.764831
16	104.767881	101.572769	98.523180
17	107.724713	104.296613	101.032487
18	110.441412	106.786856	103.315236
19	112.937482	109.063531	105.391883
20	115.230840	111.144954	107.281037

today to fund these five payments? By checking the table for the present value of 1 per period, the factor is 4.889440:

$$\$5,000 \times 4.889440 = \$24,447.20$$

To show how this deposit will be applied, we can calculate the five months of activity, remembering that each month's balance earns 9 percent interest (which is equal to 0.0075 per month):

month	*less:* payment	*plus:* interest	balance
			$24,447.20
1	$5,000.00	$183.36	19,630.56
2	5,000.00	147.23	14,777.79
3	5,000.00	110.83	9,888.62
4	5,000.00	74.16	4,962.78
5	5,000.00	37.22	0

Example: You are given the chance to lease an automobile through your company. Payments are scheduled at $325 per month for the next three years. Rather than taking the money from your personal budget, you want to put aside part of your savings to fund the lease payments. The total of payments over 36 months is $11,700; however, you will not need to deposit that much, since your account will also earn interest. If you can earn 9 percent, compounded monthly, how much must you deposit today? The 9 percent table shows a 3-year factor of 31.446805:

$$\$325.00 \times 31.446805 = \$10,220.21$$

To build your own table for the present value of 1 per period, add the factors shown on the table for the present value of 1. The steps are shown in Figure 6-12.

On a hand calculator, you can build a table with a series of additions, referring to the present value of 1 table. Follow these steps:

Figure 6-12.
Present value of 1 per period.

	9% FACTOR
add the factors on the table, present value of 1	
1st month:	0.992556

2nd month:
$$\begin{array}{r} 0.992556 \\ + 0.985167 \end{array} \quad = \quad 1.977723$$

3rd month:
$$\begin{array}{r} 1.977723 \\ + 0.977833 \end{array} \quad = \quad 2.955556$$

TABLE 9% MONTHLY	
month	factor
1	0.992556
2	1.977723
3	2.955556
4	3.926110
5	4.889440
6	5.845598

1. Enter the factor for
   the first month   0.992556
2. Depress + (add)   +
3. Enter the factor for
   the second month   0.985167
4. Depress = (total) for
   the second month's total   =
                                         1.977723
5. Depress + (add)   +

6. Repeat steps three through five for
   subsequent periods

Amortization Payments

The last table shows the amount of periodic payments
needed to pay off the balance of one dollar, given a rate of
interest and compounding method and a repayment term.
The best-known example of amortization payments is the
debt on a home mortgage that is subject to fully amortized
repayments. The factor from the table is multiplied by the
loan amount, and the resulting answer is the required payment. Figure 6-13 shows a sample page from a book of compound interest tables for amortization payments.

Example: You are writing a report that suggests the company will
benefit by purchasing equipment it is now leasing. As part of your
analysis, you must compare the cost of financing the purchase to the
amount of monthly lease payments. The purchase will require borrowing $25,000, and you assume interest will be charged at 9 percent,
compounded monthly. The repayment term will be 10 years.

To figure the amount of monthly payments, refer to a monthly
table for amortization payments. At 9 percent interest, the factor for
10 years is 0.012668:

$$\$25,000 \times 0.012668 = \$316.70$$

Two important facts are revealed. First, the monthly payment can
now be compared to lease payments, which will affect cash flow. Second, you can calculate the total amount of interest that will be paid
over 10 years. Follow these steps to calculate total interest:

1. Multiply the monthly payment by the number of months in the repayment term	$316.70 × 120
2. The answer is the total of payments	$38,004
3. Subtract the amount of the loan	− 25,000
4. The balance is the total interest expense	$13,004

Figure 6-13.
Sample interest tables for amortization payments.

	MONTHLY		
Amortization Payments			
months	*8.50%*	*9.00%*	*9.50%*
1	1.007083	1.007500	1.007917
2	0.505319	0.505632	0.505945
3	0.338067	0.338346	0.338625
4	0.254443	0.254705	0.254967
5	0.204270	0.204522	0.204775
6	0.170823	0.171069	0.171315
7	0.146933	0.147175	0.147417
8	0.129017	0.129256	0.129494
9	0.115083	0.115319	0.115555
10	0.103937	0.104171	0.104406
11	0.094818	0.095051	0.095284
years			
1	0.087220	0.087451	0.087684
2	0.045456	0.045685	0.045914
3	0.031568	0.031800	0.032033
4	0.024648	0.024885	0.025123
5	0.020517	0.020758	0.021002
6	0.017778	0.018026	0.018275
7	0.015836	0.016089	0.016344
8	0.014392	0.014650	0.014911
9	0.013279	0.013543	0.013809
10	0.012399	0.012668	0.012940
11	0.011686	0.011961	0.012239
12	0.011101	0.011380	0.011664
13	0.010612	0.010897	0.011186
14	0.010199	0.010489	0.010784
15	0.009847	0.010143	0.010442
16	0.009545	0.009845	0.010150
17	0.009283	0.009588	0.009898
18	0.009055	0.009364	0.009679
19	0.008854	0.009169	0.009488
20	0.008678	0.008997	0.009321

On average, the yearly interest cost is about $1,300. But because interest is calculated on each month's outstanding balance, interest costs are higher in the earlier years and fall as the loan is amortized.

Example: You have decided to purchase a home. However, you do not know whether your personal budget can absorb the monthly payments. In order to determine what will be required, you can use a table for the amortization of 1. Assuming you estimate you will need to finance $80,000, you want to determine whether to seek a 15-year or a 30-year loan. Referring to the table, the factors are 0.010143 (15-year term) and 0.008046 (30-year term):

15-year repayment:
$80,000 × 0.010143 = $811.44

30-year repayment:
$80,000 × 0.008046 = $643.68

Payments for the longer term are lower; however, the total interest cost is higher:

total cost, 15-year term:		
$811.44 × 180 months	=	$146,059.20
less: original loan	=	80,000.00
total interest	=	$66,059.20
total cost, 30-year term:		
$643.68 × 360 months	=	$231.724.80
less: original loan	=	80,000.00
total interest	=	$151,724.80

Accountants use amortization calculations to compute the cost of debt service on corporate liabilities, such as bank loans and bonds. The estimated interest costs are built into budgets, and principal payments are used to figure the effect of borrowing money on working capital.

In your departmental budget, in reports, and in other applications involving calculations of interest and principal, you will find many applications for the table for amortization payments. To develop your own table for amortization payments, divide 1 by the factors on the table for the present value of 1 per period. The steps in this process are shown in Figure 6-14.

On a hand calculator, follow these steps:

1. Enter 1	1
2. Depress ÷ (divide)	÷
3. Enter the factor listed in the first month on the present value of 1 per period table	0.992556
4. Depress = (total) to arrive at the factor for the first month	= 1.007500
5. Repeat for each period, using the corresponding factor on the present value of 1 table	

INTERPOLATING A FACTOR

The intensely mathematical aspects of computing the time value of money—whether to calculate accumulated value, present value, or amortization payments—point out the reasons that many managers find these procedures confusing. When you look at a book full of tables, broken down by computing methods, all of the tables seem so similar that deciding which one to use is frustrating.

Once you understand the practical applications and once you know how to build your own tables, the process becomes quite clear. Much of the math phobia that nonaccounting managers experience comes from a lack of understanding about compound interest.

However, even when you are armed with a book of compound interest tables, and you know how to use each one, you will not always be able to get the answer you need, because most books include rates for half or quarter percent-

Figure 6-14.
Amortization payments.

		9% FACTOR

**divide 1 by the factors on
the table, present value
of 1 per period**

1st month:

$$\frac{1}{0.992556} = 1.007500$$

2nd month:

$$\frac{1}{1.977723} = 0.505632$$

3rd month:

$$\frac{1}{2.955556} = 0.338346$$

TABLE 9% MONTHLY	
month	factor
1	1.007500
2	0.505632
3	0.338346
4	0.254705
5	0.204522
6	0.171069

ages only. In many situations, you will need to calculate interest at a rate somewhere in between the rates listed.

Example: You want to propose to management that a new project should be financed. However, it will be necessary to borrow $50,000. In order to write your report, you call your banker and ask for a rate quote. You are told that the loan rate as 12.625 percent. You want to figure out the monthly repayment. But your book of interest tables does not include 12.625 percent. It reports rates for 12.50 and 13.00 percent.

You can interpolate (estimate) the rate by using the table for rates above and below the rate you need. The factors for a 10-year repayment term at these rates are:

$$12.50\% = 0.014638$$
$$13.00\% = 0.014931$$

By taking an average of these two factors, you can estimate the factor for 12.75 percent, which is halfway between the two reported rates:

$$\frac{0.014638 + 0.014931}{2} = 0.014785$$

Next, the approximate factor for 12.625 percent can be interpolated, since it lies halfway between 12.50 percent (the factor known from the table) and 12.75 percent (the factor calculated above). Add these two together and divide by 2 to compute the average factor:

$$\frac{0.014638 + 0.014785}{2} = 0.014712$$

This factor can safely be used to estimate monthly payments required at the rate of 12.625 percent. The resulting answer will be correct within one dollar.

You will discover that having a familiarity with the methods for calculating the time value of money will add value to your reports, budgets, and other forms of financially oriented communications you prepare. Keeping in mind that numbers are the reporting mode of business, this skill must be considered essential.

Chapter 7 explains techniques for creating effective reports that influence action. With an improved comfort level with numbers and their use, your reports will have an added dimension, and you will be able to compete with accountants in explaining your point of view with an emphasis on profits.

Chapter 7

Creating an Effective Report

Even reports that do not include financial information invariably discuss profits or losses. A summary of employee workload, for example, must deal with the company's investment in payroll expense and the efficiency factors related to it. A report on a division's production or a department's transaction load also translates to costs, expenses, and profits.

Since discussion of financial information is unavoidable in business reports, attempting to avoid numbers within reports is futile. Some nonaccounting managers may attempt to write their reports in a purely narrative fashion, ignoring the fact that business deals with scorekeeping. In every aspect of every manager's job, the three elements of communication, influence, and planning cannot be separated from the importance of profit.

Whenever you communicate with another employee, manager, or executive, the question of profitability will eventually arise. Your communication may be verbal or written but, in either case, numbers must come into the picture. Even when the question of profit is not raised, it is always there—because business exists to create efficient means for producing profits.

REPORTING IN TERMS OF THE NUMBERS

Failing to discuss financial issues in a report has one unfortunate result: Your report lacks validity. For example, you propose that the company should invest in new equipment on the premise that it will add to your department's efficiency. However, you merely request the additional equipment. A more effective approach is to point out the problem and then demonstrate how your idea will reduce costs and add to profits.

All managers, including nonaccountants, prepare reports in many forms, and quite frequently. Letters, memos, verbal exchanges, and participation in meetings all are forms of reporting. The only difference for accountants is that many of their reports are prepared in written form. Part of the hesitation managers experience about preparing reports is the fear of putting down on paper something that might be challenged.

Dealing with numbers in reports can be a problem for accountants. They think in terms of numbers, and thus are less likely to be concerned with making their reports interesting reading matter. To confirm this, look at any financial statement. The universally accepted format consists entirely of numbers, without any interpretive information. Footnotes disclaim, explain, or expand what the numbers on the statement mean. But statements themselves hold no particular literary merit.

When you must include numbers in a report, avoid the common mistake of attempting to explain them in a narrative form. Follow this rule: Don't just list the numbers. Put them down in summary, and then explain what they mean.

Most managers, accountants included, miss the point when it comes to numbers. They report financial information but fail to explain how that affects a trend, what the numbers mean for the future, and how others should respond to the information itself.

The typical accountant's report limits itself to listings of verified financial fact. And that is the limit of the accounting function. But when it comes to a nonaccountant's job, reporting gives you the opportunity to do much more. A problem arises, however, in the way that numbers are included in many reports. Simply listing them or taking the reader's time with a lengthy narrative detailing results is not productive use of a report's space. And as most readers will give only limited time to reading what you write, you're better off making the information as valuable as possible.

    Example: A manager writes a report concerning telephone costs for the last six months as part of a budget review. The first draft reads:

> Telephone expenses for the first half rose above budgeted levels. In January, the department's expense was $312, compared with a budget of $250. February's total was $285, or $35 over budget. March telephone expenses were $247, three dollars below the budget. April reported $303, or an unfavorable variance of $53. May's telephone expense was $261, $11 over budget. And expenses in the month of June were $274, which was $24 over budget. For the entire six-month period, expenses totaled $1,682, which was $182 over budget, or an unfavorable variance of 12 percent.

This statement provides a summary of what the numbers are, but it gives the reader no indication of the problem or how to solve it. The numbers themselves should not be listed in such complete detail, but can be summarized in one sentence. Then in approximately the same amount of space, the report can be made more useful. For example:

> Telephone expenses for the six-month period totaled $1,682, compared with a budget of $1,500, or an unfavorable variance of 12 percent. The budget was based on the assumption that expenses would approximate expense levels of the previous year. However, two conditions were not anticipated. First, rates were increased by 4 percent at the beginning of the year. Second, the company began conducting business in the Eastern Division, and the rate of long-distance calls has risen.

This revised format explains the causes of the problem. It should then concentrate on recommending specific solutions. For example, a budget revision should be made to allow for increased costs. Expenses may be reduced with an 800 number, an improved phone system, or the installation of a telephone log. A report should always contain more than just the passive information. It can be expanded to advise management how to solve problems.

If the month-to-month details of the report must be included, place them in a chart and put it behind the more important explanatory section. Structure reports keeping these points in mind:

1. Few people will take the time to read an entire report. It must be put together so that the most important information appears at the top and supporting facts are left for later.
2. Telling a reader what the numbers are is of little value. Most reports lack an explanation of what the numbers reveal.
3. Never simply list a problem and let it go at that. Reports are useful only when they explain a problem in terms of how it can be solved.

BECOMING AN EFFECTIVE REPORT PREPARER

Putting ideas on paper is intimidating for several reasons. First, you know you will be judged by the statements you make, and, if you are wrong, then others will have a negative opinion of you. Second, there is the ever-present hesitation when reporting to anyone who outranks you in the organization. And third, as a nonaccounting manager, you might believe that you are not qualified to interpret facts affecting profits.

All of these fears are natural, but all are easily overcome. You will be judged by what you say, either in written or verbal reporting. So if you want to excel as a report writer, you must arm yourself with facts.

You have a great advantage in reporting on the significance of financial trends in your own department. You are in the best position to study the numbers and then draw conclusions in the context of what they mean to your department.

To make your reports effective, include the numbers but devote the body of the report to explaining what they mean. Identify and clearly express the problem, and then propose solutions, including a plan of action and a suggested deadline. Some managers will argue that reports are not necessarily done to address problems but are merely status summaries. If there is no problem, then what's the purpose of the report? This question can serve as a means for identifying reports that are not needed. Perhaps a nonproblem report can be eliminated.

WHERE MOST REPORTS FAIL

Even a status report must concern itself with solving problems. Its purpose is to spot any emerging negative trends so that action can be taken to correct them.

Example: You prepare a report each month, listing your department's budget and actual expenses. Any unfavorable variances exceeding 5 percent must be explained. As long as there are no significant unfavorable variances to explain, the status report is easily prepared, and no further comment is necessary. However, once a problem arises, it must be addressed. In most situations of this nature, an interesting reaction occurs on the part of the manager: The problem itself is replaced with the question, "How do I explain this so that the problem will go away?" Rather than researching the problem and finding its cause, the manager puts an effort into producing an explanation that will satisfy the *procedure* of variance reporting. This is one reason that reports often are useless.

A second and equally interesting response will be seen on the part of the executive who reviews the report: As long as there is an explanation, the procedure is satisfied. No action will be taken. So a status report exists for the purpose of locating emerging bad trends. However, when those trends appear, the report preparer does not identify the problems or propose solutions. Then, when the report is received, the reader, who should be responsible for reversing negative trends, is satisfied to do nothing.

If you want to make your reports useful, it will be necessary to break out of the reporting cycle as it is practiced in many companies. Satisfying a procedure is not enough.

When you find a problem in the preparation of a status report, identify it specifically and then propose solutions. A budget status report, for example, should not be thought of as adequate just because an explanation of variances is given. It should show where the flaw exists and other specific solutions to the *problem*—and not just compliance with procedure.

A report might satisfy the requirements of your job, in the sense that it is well written, neatly typed and bound, and delivered on time. But if the report does not point out problems and how they can be solved, it serves no real purpose.

THE STRUCTURE OF THE REPORT

Reports must give the reader something of value that can be acted upon and from which specific decisions can be made. A "safe" report, one that passively lists facts without any interpretation, fails in this respect.

Example: You prepare a budget report that shows an unfavorable variance of 12 percent in telephone expenses for the six months just ended. Your explanation reads, "Telephone expenses exceeded budget by 12 percent. We expect this variance to be absorbed during the third quarter." This "explanation" provides nothing of use to the executive who receives the report. The variance percentage is already known, because it shows up on the budget summary; so the first sentence is nothing more than a narrative version of financial information already presented. And the second sentence makes a claim that cannot be substantiated.

A real explanation will identify specifically why the budget was not right or why expenses went over the budget. There *is* an issue here worth discussing, one that cannot be thrown aside by implying that it's a timing problem.

Example: The marketing manager of a software manufacturing company writes a report suggesting that sales outlets should be opened in three new regions. The report discusses competition, buying trends, and marketing opportunities. It evaluates the costs and risks of expansion, identifies the cash flow problems involved with opening new offices, and projects sales and profits for one year. However, the report's organization makes it difficult to follow, and the specific recommendations are buried on page 26.

Remembering that most people will not take the time to read through a lengthy report, set a goal for yourself:

> List every report's major conclusions and recommendations on the first page.

You have considerable leeway in designing reports and in changing accepted design. Even when you are told to prepare a report in a very specific format, recommend that a revised format be used, one that serves the report's purpose in a better way.

The best format for a report is to include a summary on the first page and then to supply supporting information. All of your reports should contain major sections, as summarized in Figure 7-1:

1. Purpose and scope. Define your report. What is the purpose for writing it? What known problems does it address, and why? The purpose and scope can be summarized in one short paragraph.

2. Major conclusions. Once the purpose of your report has been listed, summarize your conclusions. This summary may require only one sentence, or it might take a longer paragraph.

3. Recommendations. List the specific actions you recommend. On the first page, keep these to single sentences and leave the details for later. From this one page, the reader grasps the whole story in moments. The scope, purpose, problem, and suggested solutions are included together. Now, if the reader wants to question your conclusions, the body of the report, which is the last section, supplies the answers. The body includes both narrative sections and financial summaries. The first backup section should include an

Figure 7-1.
Report structure.

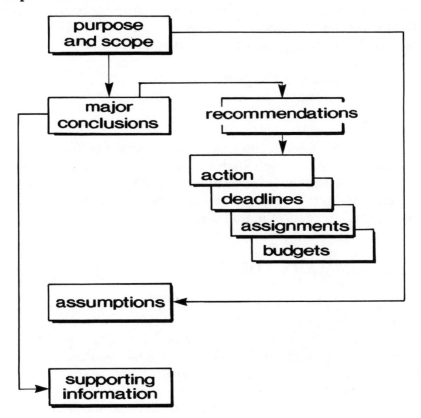

expansion of your recommendations, including four components:

- Action. List the actions you recommend to implement
  your recommendations.
- Deadlines. Propose dates for completing the actions
  you propose.
- Assignments. Suggest responsibility for executing actions and meeting deadlines.
- Budgets. If your recommendations involve spending
  money, show how that expense represents an investment in future profits.

4. *Assumptions.* After expanding on your recommendations, the rest of the report should be concerned with details.
First is a section that explains the assumptions used to state
the purpose and scope of the report. You must base several
points of your report on assumptions, including:

- The nature of the problem
- Management's priorities for solutions
- What's required for a solution

5. *Supporting information.* A final section is for supporting information, which includes worksheets, facts and figures, and historical information, all backing up your major
conclusion. In this section, also include any information that
supports your recommendations.

THE SUMMARY FORM

One way to force immediate response, in agreement or not,
is to clearly state your recommendations. In any business
report, these should be put on that all-important first page,
where there can be no mistake about what you are suggesting. It's a mistake to hedge your arguments, to scatter your
recommendations throughout the pages, or to leave them
until the end. Another mistake is to depend too heavily on
strictly financial information. It is difficult to comprehend
columns and rows of numbers when a brief narrative explanation can better highlight your key points. Leave the detailed financial listings for the supporting information in the
back of the report. The important points that must be raised
should be shown in brief, direct summaries.

Even a report that depends heavily on financial information can be made informative and easy to read. In some
reports, there are so many numbers that little room is left
for explanation. In these cases, use the summary and detail
format.

The summary and detail format calls for a brief listing
of the key financial facts, perhaps boxed off near the front of

the report and included there only for the purpose of discussion and explanation. The more detailed information that makes up those summaries is included in a later section.

Keep this point in mind:

> Whenever you find yourself using more numbers than narrative, it's time to look for ways to summarize.

Whenever you use the summary and detail method, be sure that your report is properly cross-referenced. The reader will have to be told where details are located for each summary section, and detail sections must be referenced back to the summaries they support. Place a short cross-reference note at the top of each page, so that the reader knows where else to look.

Figure 7-2 shows a summary of key financial information, and then lists the three detail sections of the report that provide more information. The advantage to this reporting format is that, for most readers, the first page and related summaries are the only sections of interest. However, if any questions do arise, cross-references are included and finding most answers will be an easy task. For those readers who want more than the summary provides, the format is just as easy to use.

ANNOTATION AND FOOTNOTES

The problems of presenting information on the first page are compounded when your report is especially complex. You may need a good deal of self-editing to summarize your report in a few lines. And when much financial information must be included in the sections supporting recommendations or listing assumptions, even a clearly written report can confuse rather than enlighten the reader.

Two techniques will help you to overcome obstacles to communicating as clearly as possible: the use of annotation and footnotes. When information must be qualified or ex-

Figure 7-2.
Summary and detail.

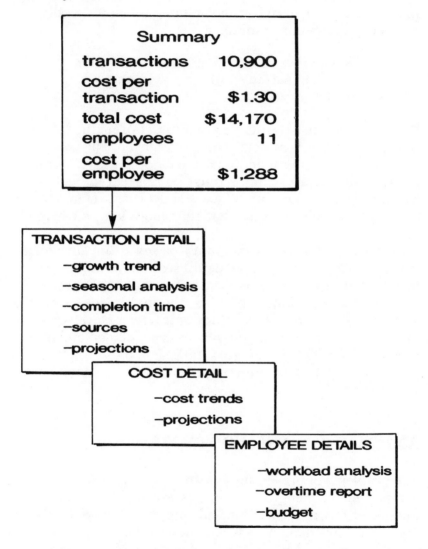

Summary

transactions	10,900
cost per transaction	$1.30
total cost	$14,170
employees	11
cost per employee	$1,288

TRANSACTION DETAIL

-growth trend

-seasonal analysis

-completion time

-sources

-projections

COST DETAIL

-cost trends

-projections

EMPLOYEE DETAILS

-workload analysis

-overtime report

-budget

plained beyond the mere presentation of numbers, these two devices will help you to clarify, without distracting the reader.

Example: In the body of your report, you must explain four months of expenses as part of your departmental budget. The third month includes a three-month adjustment for expenses allocated to your department, which created a large, unexpected budget variance. And the fourth month does not include expenses for the final week, as the month was not closed off by the deadline.

That's a lot of explanation for what would otherwise be a straightforward listing of four months' expenses. Figure 7-3 shows how a brief chart can be expanded with the use of annotation.

Footnoting will work for a somewhat longer explanation or can be used in place of annotation. Figure 7-4 shows how the same brief chart can be left uncluttered, with the needed explanations placed below.

Figure 7-3.
Annotation format.

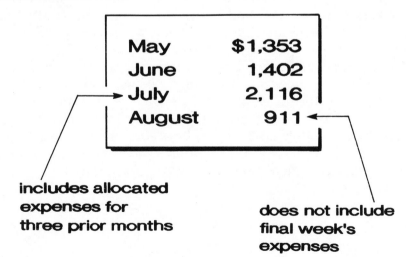

Figure 7-4.
Footnoted format.

May	$1,353
June	1,402
July (1)	2,116
August (2)	911

(1) includes allocated
    expenses for three
    prior months

(2) does not include final
    week's expenses

Avoid overusing annotation, footnoting, and any other form of exception to straight paragraph form in the narrative sections of your reports. Excessive use of these qualifying devices will become difficult to follow and tedious to track. But appropriate and limited application of these ideas certainly helps to achieve the desired simplicity and flow of a report.

In some instances, graphic treatment of material can simplify a message that could never be as clearly expressed in narrative form, even with appropriate annotation and footnoting. Yet, many reports that could benefit greatly from the inclusion of charts and graphs are never expanded to include these valuable tools. Chapter 8 shows how anyone can construct a simple but informative report graphic.

Chapter 8

Graphics in Reports

Everyone who prepares a report must deal with the problem of expressing financial information in a clear and uncluttered manner. This task is difficult when your report contains a lot of numbers. Simple charts and graphs can make all the difference. This chapter addresses the problem of communicating financial information in recurring reports. The graphics presented are not difficult to construct, and with a few supplies and some practice, any manager can add a good deal of value to any report.

The two aids for simplifying information in a report are the chart and the graph. A chart highlights information, whereas a graph shows changes over time or a comparison between two or more factors. For example, a chart would be used to show the total quarterly expense levels in your department. A graph would present the same financial information on a scale (top to bottom) over time (left to right).

A chart or graph can be designed using the underline key on a typewriter or word processing program, or it can be drawn with a pencil or pen. There is no need for a special drafting tool, although rapidiograph pens do draw more consistently than others.

Graphs should be constructed on grid paper, with the grids printed in light blue (this will not be picked up in most photocopying or printing processes). Besides the lines you will need in charts and graphs, you will need to add words for titles, captions, and legends. A simple graph can be done on a typewriter, or for a better appearance, sheets of various sizes and styles of rub-on letters can be purchased at a local art store.

The beginning kit for making your own high-quality

graphs can be as simple as a ruler, a high-quality pen, and a typewriter with a new ribbon. Or, to expand your graphics, you should also consider buying a drafting pen, a supply of press-on letters, and grid paper. All that you will need to produce very high-quality business charts and graphs will cost less than $50 and should be adequate to produce thirty to forty graphs, perhaps more. The actual use will depend on how complex your graphic reporting becomes.

VARIATIONS IN GRAPHICS

You can improve a financial report simply by setting aside certain important information and presenting it in a boxed-off area. This simplified chart highlights the key points that your reader will need to know. A simple chart can be prepared on a typewriter and then boxed off for emphasis:

> Observation: A chart is most often used to summarize financial information. However, don't overlook the use of a chart to draw your reader's attention to a key point. This paragraph is an example of such a chart.

All visual aids should be kept as simple as possible. If you include too much information on one graphic, you will confuse the reader rather than clarify your point. Don't forget the primary reason for reducing certain information to graphic form: A chart or graph should uncomplicate your report, enabling the reader to quickly find and understand your message in a visual form.

Don't load your report with a variety of different charts and graphs. Using too many different formats could also give your report a disconnected and disorganized character.

Some guidelines for preparing graphics:

1. Use them only to highlight or to simplify. A graphic is appropriate only when it communicates more clearly and more efficiently than narrative.

2. Try to place a graphic on the same page as the section discussing the same topic or as close to it as possible. Avoid putting an appendix of charts and graphs in the back of the report, forcing the reader to flip back and forth. Remember that comprehension will be at its highest when the reader can read and see information at the same time.
3. Keep the task simple. Use technology that allows you to create professional visual aids with a minimum of time and expense.
4. Never take up narrative room to tell the reader what the numbers are. Instead, show the financial information in a chart or graph, and use narrative to explain what they mean.

CREATING CHARTS

Most visual aids you use in reports are varieties of the chart. A strictly narrative report is of limited value to a reader because it demands time to find information and to then understand what it means. Even the most routine report can be improved when some information is set aside and highlighted.

The chart is a table that is enclosed or set apart from other sections of the report. It can be placed between paragraphs as a separate section on a page, or it can be enclosed within a paragraph, like the example to the right. Both formats are acceptable, although the in-text version may prove to be more difficult to work with if your report will be typed by someone else or is subject to change in editing.

Charts are most useful in long narrative sections of reports. It is very difficult to read anything that explains a situation in detail, especially when cost and other financial infor-

	heading
. . . . .	\$. . . .
. . . . .	. . . .
. . . . .	. . . .
. . . . .	. . . .
. . . . .	. . . .
total	\$. . . .

mation is involved. The simple chart not only breaks up the otherwise monotonous report, it also draws the reader from one point to the next. In addition, breaking out financial information helps you maintain a smooth flow in your narrative sections. Reports are very difficult to read when the points you want to make are constantly interrupted with a digression to financial information. Put the numbers aside and allow your narrative to flow more smoothly.

You may use a number of simple chart variations based primarily on the method of boxing off. Some chart variations are shown in Figure 8-1. A single or double line surrounding all of the information is the most standard format and is one of the easiest to construct. Beyond that, charts can be made more pleasing to look at by adding a moderate degree of perspective.

THE LINE GRAPH

While charts are intended to highlight or summarize information, graphs are summarized representations of information, presented on a scaled-down version. Comprehending a list of numbers is difficult for everyone, and a visual summary presents the same information very quickly. The typical best use of a graph is to explain financial information visually when a mere listing of numbers cannot achieve the task as well.

Graphs come in several different forms. The simplest of these is the line graph, a single line going from left to right (representing time), and varying from top to bottom (representing value). The value/time format of the line graph is standard and is widely understood and used in business. This graph is most appropriate for reporting a *single* factor, or for comparing no more than two comparable factors. For example, a sales manager might use a line graph to show the number of sales calls made during the year, or a production supervisor might use one to track the number of units produced by each shift by day.

Figure 8-1.
Variations of the chart.

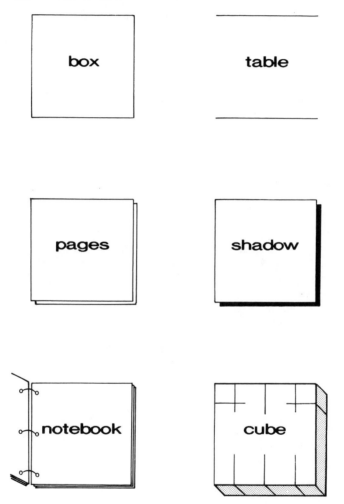

Figure 8-2(a) shows a line graph in which six months of sales volume are reported in a range between $200,000 and approximately $400,000 per month.

Note that the shape of the graph is approximately square. If your graph is more rectangular, it should favor length over height. Avoid creating graphs that are too high or too long, even if that means constructing a scale that pro-

Figure 8-2.
The line graph.

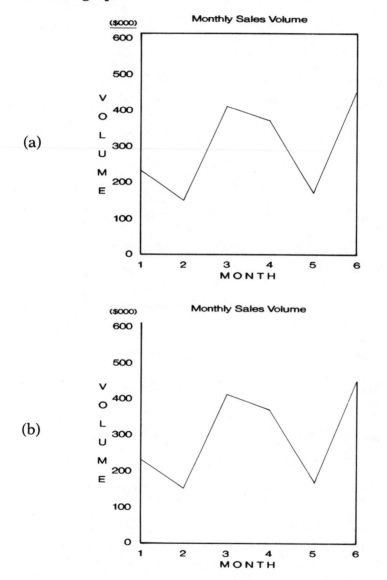

Figure 8-2. *(continued)*

(c)

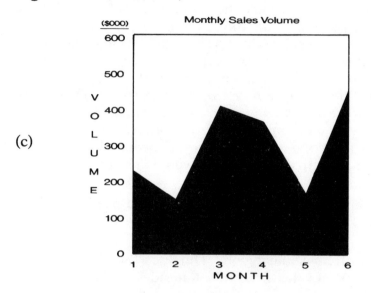

vides more value area than you need. In this case, the reporting period was six months. To achieve the desired shape, it was necessary to construct the graph with approximately six value segments. Increments of $100,000 were selected, even though the actual sales range did not require all of that space.

Guidelines for selecting the right scale:

1. Devise a scale that approximates a square or slightly rectangular shape.
2. When building more than one related graph in your report, strive for consistency in scale. Using different scales may distort the information.
3. Always begin value scaling at zero; otherwise, the significance of change will be lost. For example, if a sales graph starts out with the value of $200,000 rather than zero, the lower months will appear to be severe declines, rather than in-range changes.
4. Always use equal increments between value and time, to ensure accurate change reporting. For ex-

ample, if you report in increments of 100 from top to bottom, don't vary those increments for 75, 50, and 25. Keep the scale the same throughout the graph.

5. Always label your graph clearly. Don't expect the reader to know that value is reported from top to bottom and time from left to right.
6. Include a caption or title with every graph you prepare, even when it is clearly explained in text.
7. Use legends, annotation, or footnoting to clarify and explain the graph. However, avoid cluttering the graph with extra material you don't need.

The graph in Figure 8-2(a) is squared off on all sides, with a single, solid line drawn in. Two variations of this are:

1. Limited squaring-off. Outside lines are always drawn for the time and value sides, and a partial line is included only to the extent of the final value. This form of the line graph is shown in Figure 8-2(b).
2. Highlighted value. The graph is prepared in the same way as Figure 8-2(a) but the area beneath the value line is blackened, as shown in Figure 8-2(c).

EXPANDING THE LINE GRAPH

Line graphs can be used to compare two related forms of information and can save a great deal of narrative explanation that would be needed without the visual aid. Figure 8-3 shows a sales graph that was prepared in the same manner as Figure 8-2. But in addition to a visual summary of the trend, the forecast totals are included as well.

Besides communicating the point simply and clearly, your graphs must be easy to read. When more than one form of information is shown on your line graph, be sure to include a legend. In Figure 8-3, the legend shows that the actual sales are indicated by a solid line, and the forecast sales are indicated by a dotted line.

Figure 8-3.
Comparative line graph.

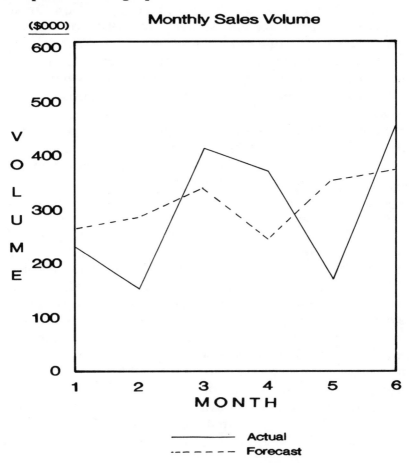

Don't expect your graphs to stand alone. Devote adequate narrative space to pointing out the significant conclusions that should be drawn from the graphic summaries.

In the case of the sales comparison, the typical forecast
and budget report would take space to explain the results.
But once that is reduced to a graph, the same space can be
used to point out what it all means. For example, you might
conclude from the graph that, while sales forecasting was
accurate on average, it did not allow for seasonal changes.

Some of the reported variation might be significant enough for you to recommend a review and change in forecasting procedures. You can add value to reporting by taking an active role as interpreter and analyst and not being satisfied with a passive summary of the numbers.

In addition to reporting two related forms of information on one graph, it might be necessary to use two different scales. For example, the two types of information you are reporting are measured in different ways; however, you want to show them on the same graph, because changes in each are closely related. A two-scaled graph is more difficult to comprehend. But at the same time, the need to report on related trends might make it necessary.

If you must use two separate scales, construct the graph so that the left and right sides do not cross over. This can be accomplished by planning the scale carefully. In Figure 8-4, the total units of production (left scale) are compared to the percentage of defects (right scale). The one value involves numbers, and the other involves percentages. Thus, the two scales are necessary. The significance of the trend could not be demonstrated clearly if two separate graphs were used.

A two-scaled graph must always include a legend so that the meaning is as clear as possible. In Figure 8-4, the units of production are shown in the solid line and the percentage of defects is shown with the broken line.

If you must report information that involves comparisons of more than two related factors, avoid the line graph. While this may be the easiest graph to construct, it will not always be the most appropriate.

THE BAR GRAPH

Virtually all forms of financial information gain significance *only* when reported in comparison. That's why so much of the accounting information you hear is expressed in percentage increases or decreases from the prior period, as a percentage over or under the budget, or as a numerical value shown next to the same information from last year.

Figure 8-4.
The two-scaled line graph.

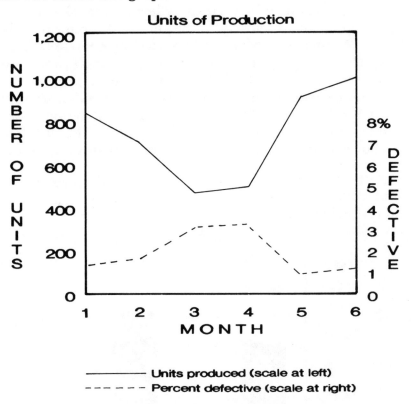

Units produced (scale at left)
- - - - - Percent defective (scale at right)

Example: You are preparing a report on annual production in four separate divisions, as part of a regional analysis. You want to show each region's total production in a comparative format.

Using a line graph for a report such as this would be confusing if a month-to-month sales trend is being reported. You would need four separate trend lines, and they would probably cross over. A second problem is that the trend line will not report the information you need. You want to show the final production figure, not the month-to-month change.

A bar graph is appropriate for reporting final results for a number of comparable facts (divisions, departments, companies, etc.). Rather than showing the action of change, the bar graphs report results for a period of time or the status as of a specific date.

Bar graphs may be vertical or horizontal. The vertical bar graph conforms closely to the standardized form of the line graph, since the values are reported from top to bottom. However, in a bar graph, the left-to-right time factor is replaced with a stationary distinction. For example, the four divisions are compared not over time, but for the entire year. Figure 8-5 shows a vertical bar graph in which the value side represents the number of new orders placed. The divisions are shown separately along the bottom. For this example, a

Figure 8-5.
The vertical bar graph.

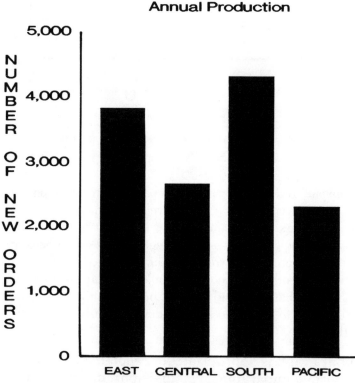

line graph would be of little use, since you are not concerned as much with changes over time as with the final outcome.

The vertical bar graph can be prepared on a comparative basis for each of the four divisions, without overly complicating it. For example, assume you want to show both the number of new orders actually generated and the number projected in the year's forecast. A comparative vertical bar graph for this information is shown relatively simply in Figure 8-6. It expresses the year's outcome immediately and allows the reader to see at a glance how well divisions have lived up to expectations. East and South divisions exceeded their projections, while Central and Pacific came in under forecast.

As with all cases of comparative reporting, a legend is included, so that the reader can identify exactly what the graph reports. In Figure 8-6, actual figures are shown in black and the projected numbers are shaded.

When the bar graph must compare a greater number of results, the horizontal format is more practical. Although any form of information can be shown vertically, it is not always the clearest alternative.

Example: The comparison between divisions must be done not just for one year but over a three-year period. On the same graph you want to show the three-year results for all four divisions. The clearest way to achieve this result is to use a horizontal bar graph similar to Figure 8-7.

THE CIRCLE GRAPH

The most difficult graph to prepare is the circle graph (also called the pie chart). It communicates information in a very clear manner, but it also has limited applications. The circle graph is useful only when reporting a single and stationary factor. For example, it would not be useful for showing sales by quarter or for breaking down the number of orders by division.

Figure 8-6.
The comparative vertical bar graph.

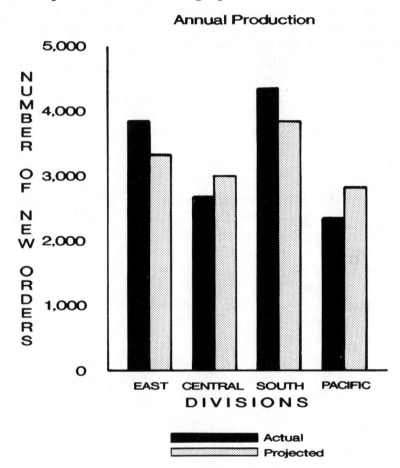

Often used to illustrate spending, a circle graph can be used only to show the components of an assumed, well-understood whole. For example, one insurance company uses the circle graph to show how the average premium dollar is spent, a consumer's group shows how the federal budget is broken down by major areas of spending, or a company shows how the average dollar of revenue is spent during the previous year.

Figure 8-7.
The horizontal bar graph.

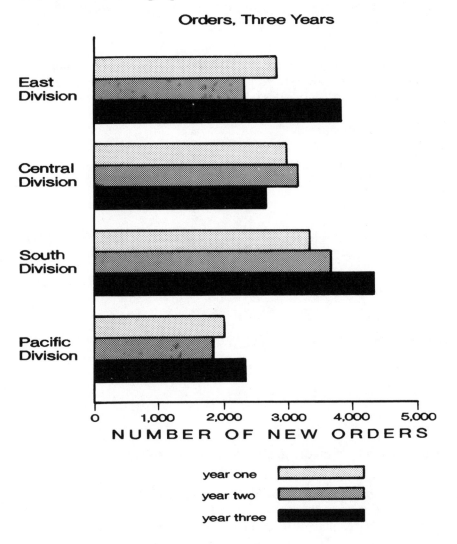

To construct a circle graph, you need a compass and a protractor. To break down the assumed 100 percent of the circle into its segments, the protractor is used to convert percentages to degrees.

Example: You are reporting on the previous year's income and spending, and you want to prepare a circle graph. The average dollarof revenue was assigned to the following categories.

Direct costs	63%
Selling expenses	24%
General and administrative expenses	11%
Net profit	2%
Total	100%

Since the full circle contains 360 degrees, these percentage breakdowns must be converted, rounding off to the closest degree:

Percent		*Circle*		*Degrees*
63	×	360	=	227
24	×	360	=	86
11	×	360	=	40
2	×	360	=	7
100				360

To construct a circle graph, follow these steps:

1. Draw the circle, allowing enough space to annotate the segments.
2. Draw a line, the base line, from the exact center of the circle to any point on its rim.
3. Place the protractor on the circle so that it lines up on the base line, and locate the degree for your first segment. Mark that point outside of the circle.
4. Draw a line from the center to the rim, lined up with the mark made for the segment.

Figure 8-8.
The circle graph.

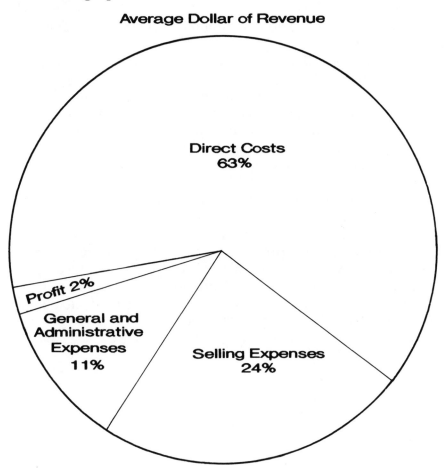

Average Dollar of Revenue

5. Using the line drawn in step 4 as your new base line, place the protractor on the circle and find the degree for your second segment. Mark that spot.
6. Repeat steps 4 and 5 until all segments have been drawn.

An example of the completed circle graph is shown in Figure 8-8.

Whichever form of graphics you decide to use in your reports, keep these key points in mind:

1. Visual aids belong in financial reports and add value to them.
2. High-quality graphs are not difficult or time-consuming to construct.
3. You will not need to delay your report by depending on a graphics department in your company if you master the skills within your own department.
4. The materials needed for hand-drawn graphics can be purchased with a very limited budget.

The purpose of graphics in your report must be to present information in its best possible format. You will gain an advantage in reporting quality by using visual aids.

Perhaps more intimidating than the written financial report is the verbal report. When you're called upon to make a presentation in a meeting, preparation and a thorough knowledge of your information are the critical elements. This subject is discussed in Chapter 9.

Chapter 9

The Verbal Report

Meetings are not always the productive, essential work sessions that they should be. However, by learning how to make a verbal presentation with comfort, you can turn a meeting into a forum for making specific decisions and formulating a course of action, get ideas approved, and increase your comfort with the idea of speaking out. This chapter provides specific ideas for improving presentation style, organizing material, and feeling comfortable in the business meeting.

REPORTING HURDLES

Many nonaccounting managers perceive reporting in the business meeting as a negative experience. Even when the accounting department is not present, the meeting leader or facilitator is likely to use the accountant's arguments to reject your ideas or conclusions. This practice is not necessarily deceptive; it comes more from force of habit than from conviction.

Example: During a meeting you present your proposal for a plan that will require the company to spend money. The leader rejects your plan with one of these arguments:

1. *The money is not in the budget.* This argument assumes that the company's budget has validity and actually serves as a management tool. You know, however, that budgets are not really used for their intended purpose. Still, this argument is very difficult to refute, since it's so final.
2. *The timing isn't right.* This argument also assumes that, in

133

some way, actions are truly planned and scheduled. But this argument might be used as a way to reject any new idea.

3. *We can't decide without a financial analysis.* This argument implies that Accounting must be involved in the decision and assumes knowledge that the accountant might not have. But management often defers to accountants with this assumption.

When you put a good deal of work into developing an idea, only to have it dismissed with one of the standard excuses, it's understandable that you will become discouraged. However, there are solutions. Your task is to structure your report so that a favorable decision and approval are inevitable.

You must expect others to question your ideas and even to reject them without hearing all of your arguments. It's human nature to resist change in any form. Remember that the key to unlocking management's resistance is:

> The organization is run by the profit motive. To win your point, you must demonstrate how your idea will increase profits—without doubt.

As long as you present your information so that this point is made, you will get through all of the arguments, often with ease. If any of the stock rejection answers are brought up, get around them with your proof.

Example: Your department now makes about 600 photocopies per month, using a machine one floor above yours. But that machine breaks down frequently, meaning work is delayed. And employees in your department often must wait up to fifteen minutes for the machine to become free. By calculating the idle time, your report proves that purchasing a photocopy machine for your department will reduce this expense, thus improving profits.

You begin to present your report, and at once, the accountant states: "We can't buy another photocopy machine this year. It's not in the budget."

This would normally be the end of the discussion. But at this step, you assume the role of manager/diplomat and present your best argument: "I understand. But if it were not for that fact, would you have a problem with the idea of increasing profits?"

Regardless of how the accountant replies to this point, you must be ready to present facts. Your report must demonstrate—beyond any doubt—that buying a new photocopy machine will reduce overtime in your department, ensure prompt completion of work, and actually improve your department's budget for the year.

Once you present your facts, you will be able to state that there is room in the budget for approval of your idea. Because approval will reduce expenses, management cannot possibly reject your idea. If they do, they're ignoring the facts.

Essential to this process is the idea that, before you ask for anything, before you state your position, and before you present conclusions, you must be armed with the indisputable facts you need. By making your case, you are operating on the professional level that management often assumes only the accounting department can achieve. It's your job to prove that you also possess the perspective and discipline to express yourself in financial terms.

Besides using the budget as an excuse to reject your ideas, accountants or meeting leaders might use one of the other common arguments. To counter them, always refer to the logic of your argument.

For example, you present your idea and are told, "The timing isn't right." In response, summarize your facts and reply, "I know that timing is essential, and it might appear that this decision should wait. However, these facts prove that the timing is right. By acting as soon as possible, we will increase profits this year."

When your idea is rejected with the argument that a financial analysis must first be done, your response should be, "Well, I'm glad we're taking that approach, because we already have the financial analysis. It's here in the report, and it proves we'll cut expenses by approving this idea."

REPORTING: THE ASSIGNMENT

To show how verbal reports can be given to get the results you want, assume your assignment is to present an idea during a meeting involving the company spending money not in the budget. Your task is to prove that your recommendation is worthwhile.

To achieve this, you must be prepared to deal with profits in a direct manner, demonstrate your understanding of every issue from the executive point of view, and present information in a highly summarized, clear manner. Details are mundane, even when they support your case. Leave them to the written report that backs up your verbal presentation.

One problem nonaccounting managers run into time and again is that Accounting may interpret the same facts differently.

Example: You present a report asking for an additional staff member in your department. Based on increasing workload and anticipating an upcoming high-volume season, you make your best case for increasing the staff. But the accountant questions your figures and suggests to management that your idea should be rejected on the basis that your facts don't mean what you claimed.

In anticipation of this argument, you must base your conclusions on facts that the accounting department cannot dispute. Interpreting facts differently than your method is not necessarily an intentional slight to you. Accountants look at information on a purely financial level; you are aware of concerns beyond the numbers.

Facts that the accountant cannot argue with include:

1. *Black-and-white truth.* This group of facts includes the actual cost of goods and services: salaries, equipment costs, and expenses.

2. *Accounting estimates.* Your best argument for estimates you include in your report is that the accounting department developed the figures. That's why, whenever possible, support your ideas with information from fi-

nancial statements, forecasts, and budgets developed by Accounting.

3. *Well-documented analysis.* Never go into a meeting with "facts" in hand that you cannot prove. If you research and conclude, you must be prepared to prove your point. For example, during your presentation, you make the statement, "The material cost is $5,000." The accountant responds, "No, it's much higher than that." At this point, be prepared to produce estimates, catalog prices, notes from phone conversations, or other forms of documented proof to support your statement.

Approach your assignment to give a verbal report by assuming that everything you claim will be challenged. And remember that in most cases, your credibility will not be questioned to your face. You must also prepare for the more common situation: You present a report, management thanks you and promises to study what you've proposed, and the meeting adjourns. Later, the decision maker meets with the accountant and asks for an opinion. Only then does the accountant criticize your report and recommend a rejection.

In this case, you're not given the chance to argue your point. You are rejected without the chance to make your case. Management probably doesn't believe it's being devious in this method; they have simply gotten used to the idea of trusting their financial advisors more than they trust the average manager.

In addition to presenting clear factual information in your report, you must address the question of risk. If you give a report that supposes profits will be increased, someone could argue, "That's a good point, but if it doesn't work out, we'll lose money." Be prepared to demonstrate how and why your idea contains no risk. Business ventures may be designed to take calculated risks but, as they grow, tend to become more conservative. One of the most popular arguments against action is that it's too risky. Dispel the risk question by building your facts, to prove that no risk exists. Or, if there is risk, address it and provide guidelines for dealing with it.

Example: You propose hiring an additional staff member and make a strong case proving the company will save more than it spends (from reduction of overhead, ability to handle a greater workload, and a combination of other factors). But the accountant argues, "What if we don't see the volume you're projecting? In that case, we'll be stuck with higher payroll costs. It's too risky."

Your best response to this argument is to refer to the accounting department's own numbers. Chances are, that department prepared the income forecast for the year. State that your estimates of workload and overtime are based on Accounting's projections. It's doubtful the accountant will admit to flaws in the forecast, meaning you create an ally to your projections.

During the preparation phase of your verbal report, always plan for the rejection of your position, and build your case with these guidelines, which are also summarized in Figure 9-1.

Figure 9-1.
Comparative guidelines.

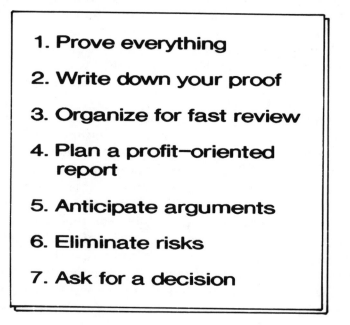

1. Prove everything

2. Write down your proof

3. Organize for fast review

4. Plan a profit-oriented report

5. Anticipate arguments

6. Eliminate risks

7. Ask for a decision

1. Prove everything. As you research a situation, always approach it from the profit motive viewpoint. Every issue must concern itself with management's unspoken question: How much is this going to cost or save? All of your facts should be included by source, so that any questions of validity can be immediately answered.

2. Write down your proof. A verbal report cannot succeed just on the basis of your words, even when you have a solid case. You must back up your verbal report with a written summary.

3. Organize for fast review. Apply the guidelines for written reports, showing your major summary and conclusions on the first page. Emphasize profits. Use the same format as a guide for your verbal report.

4. Plan a profit-oriented report. In organizing for your verbal report, always plan to present information with emphasis on increased profits. That must be presented at the top, because chances are, you'll have a limited amount of time to make your best case.

5. Anticipate arguments. Design your report to address and, thus, defuse the common arguments you expect to be made against your idea. If "it's not in the budget," raise that point and then show why the budget supports your plan. Also raise the timing issue and dispel it. And make sure you label the numbers section of your written report "financial analysis" (or a name similar to that), so that argument will be done away with at once.

6. Eliminate risks. Identify the risks your proposal brings up. Raise those risks in your report and propose how to deal with them. And when a perceived risk is unlikely to materialize, say so and explain why.

7. Ask for a decision. Meetings are frustrating because, in many companies, they are not designed for decision and action. Issues may be raised and discussed, without any results. In your report, propose a deadline and ask management for a decision.

PRESENTATION METHODS

The way in which you present your verbal report should depend on two factors: who is present at the meeting, and the nature of the report itself. If your meeting consists of a few managers gathered to discuss problems and develop solutions together, your report can be presented in a relatively informal manner. You mention the highlights: definition of the problem, your recommendations, savings, course of action, and the deadline you suggest.

If the meeting is more formal, the method of presenting material must be altered. For example, you attend a meeting in which a long agenda is controlled by the chairman of the board. Each speaker is given only a few moments, and after each segment, a number of specific questions are asked. In this higher-pressure forum, you must be prepared to summarize greatly, to respond directly and to the point, and to emphasize your key arguments.

The material you include in your verbal report will also affect your method of presentation. Reports other than one that requests a decision for the company to spend money might include:

1. The status report. The status report is a brief update on a subject or project. Keep in mind that management needs to hear the most important information first: Is the project, budget, or other matter on course, ahead of course, or behind? If behind, why? And what actions are being taken (or are suggested) to reverse negative trends?

Example: You present a monthly report summarizing the status of several ongoing projects. Your report should emphasize only those projects that are running behind schedule, why that has occurred, and what is being done to reverse the trend. You might state that the remainder of projects are on track, and nothing more needs to be said. If there are no problems to report, you can conclude very quickly. Your verbal report should run no longer than necessary.

2. The special situation report. A nonrecurring report is an opportunity to demonstrate your creativity and insight. With a report given in an acceptable form, or that recurs each month, you are limited to the accepted norm, often when you have ideas about how it could be better presented. A special situation, in comparison, is not restricted by precedent. For example, you have the opportunity to design a reporting format especially well suited to the subject at hand, to make a verbal presentation with the use of charts and graphs, and to arrange the order of your report as you want.

3. Financial report. Perhaps the greatest difficulty you will encounter is reporting on profit and loss, sales trends, and other purely financial information. If you do not have an accounting background, you might be intimidated presenting financial information during a meeting in which an accountant is present, you might hesitate to interpret the numbers in terms of what they mean to your department and to the company, and you might be unsure of how to present conclusions.

All of these doubts are addressed by taking the methodical approach to analysis that accountants use as a matter of habit. There's no special secret to this; it's just common sense. You know more about your department than your boss, the accountant, or the president of the company. Depend on your expertise, research and document everything thoroughly, and present information in the order that best expresses your conclusions. Don't be overly concerned with the need to conform to "acceptable" formats or standards in a financial report.

ANSWERING QUESTIONS

Everyone called upon to give a verbal report worries about the very act of speaking out and about being challenged by the accountant or someone else in a meeting. Every manager must also face the inevitable questions that are likely to come from others after the presentation is done. You fear that someone will ask you a question to which you don't know the answer. No one wants to show his or her ignorance. So some have attempted to talk their way through a question, rather than admitting they don't have an answer. Without exception, whenever someone attempts this, everyone else in the meeting sees through it.

A key point to remember, not just in meetings, but in every business situation, is:

> When you don't know the answer to a question, say you don't know; and then promise to find the answer.

There's no fault in admitting you don't know, especially when you promise to get an answer and report back later. This shows self-assurance. You cannot be expected to anticipate and research every possible question you'll be asked in a meeting; you can only cover a topic as completely as possible then field questions as they arise.

Do not concern yourself with the possibility that someone will ask you a hostile question. If that does occur, stick to the facts you've prepared as part of your report. Remember: The facts are at issue, not the political power plays that might surface in meetings.

When you are asked questions, be aware that some people speak up during meetings not to get information, but for other reasons: to impress their boss, to make power statements, or because they feel threatened by the proposal you offer, for example. In these cases, the less effort you put into answering a question, the better. Don't let someone else pressure you into defending your position; your facts will do that for you.

MAKING THE RIGHT IMPRESSION

Impressing others and gaining prestige and influence within the company does not result from verbal stances, at least not in the same degree that good work does. As long as your reports are thorough, correct, and oriented to corporate profits, you will gain the reputation you want and deserve. Your focus should be on the three goals every manager should strive for: to communicate, to influence, and to plan. You communicate well in a verbal report when your facts are straight, indisputable, and well presented. You influence when your ideas *must* be approved because there's no doubt about the proof supporting your conclusions. You plan by preparing well for the report in the first place and by making recommendations that anticipate the future for your company. All of these goals, when achieved, create the impression on others that you are capable of dealing with even the most difficult issues with your reports, with foresight, and with a grasp of management's concerns.

When you approach your task with a professional and well-focused attitude, you do not need to defend yourself or to resort to the political intrigues that are too often practiced in some companies. And, because you'll be concentrating on doing your job, you won't have time to participate in less productive activities.

Your written and verbal reports will be more clearly focused when they are expressed in the context of the company's plan. Planning is often a time-consuming exercise with little or no follow-up. Chapter 10 shows you how to use planning techniques to maintain focus and direction.

Chapter 10

Business Planning

The plan is a company's road map, its definition of purpose and course. But it's only as good as the actions you and other managers can take to turn the idea into a reality. Whether your company's plan exists on paper or just in the mind of management, it can succeed only if a means for monitoring the plan is devised, implemented, and reviewed.

Creating a plan is only the start. In too many instances, great effort is put into defining and writing the so-called business plan, only to abandon it during the year. This chapter shows how a companywide plan is developed and monitored and how the same principles can be applied on the departmental level.

THE COMPANY PLAN

Some managers hear the word "plan" and immediately think "budget." In many companies, these are one and the same. But in fact, budgets are only part of the broader and more comprehensive plan and planning process (see Chapter 11). It's important to realize that a budget works best only *after* a plan has been devised and conveyed to everyone in the company.

A plan is a strategic document. It should include the company's marketing objective, method of expansion and financing, and identification of new customers, territories, and product or service bases. The plan may be drawn up to attract new investors, to obtain outside financing, or to explain the company's strength and operational philosophy to customers and vendors.

All of these purposes to a plan are valid and important to management. But the plan also provides an essential opportunity for controlling and monitoring the future. Just as budgets give you the means for anticipating and even controlling future growth and profits, the plan should be designed to control change on several levels.

Example: The budget, as part of the plan, supports a number of financial assumptions made by management. But the current marketing plan identifies a new and potentially large market. To penetrate that market, the company needs to invest in:

- Greater payroll expense
- Larger home office and warehouse facilities
- Capital equipment and machinery

Much more is involved in making a marketing plan work than just a budget and forecast. Top management must time and coordinate the phases of expansion, assess the risks involved in making a move, and bring middle management into the planning and implementation phases.

Unfortunately, some companies experience great difficulty in periods of expansion, even to the extent that they lose money rather than realize a profit. One reason for this is that middle management—where the action must occur for a plan to succeed—often is left in the dark, rather than being treated as the critical link in an expansion plan.

Even with the best intentions, top management might depend too heavily on counsel from their accountant and become overly preoccupied with the financial side of expansion to the exclusion of nonfinancial planning demands. Thus, expansion is attempted with inadequate personnel, facilities, and capital assets.

This flaw is not an accounting fault. It's top management's responsibility to include the essential departmental leadership in planning and implementing a plan. Accounting cannot be expected to coordinate a marketing strategy, internal recruitment and training, and the purchase of larger systems to handle increased volume. Its specialty is financial. So when the CEO brings the chief accountant into a meeting and asks for an analysis of the plan, the response is likely to emphasize financial problems and solutions.

Top management should take responsibility for establishing the course of expansion. Admittedly, Accounting is probably the appropriate place for development of much of the planning document. But beyond that, other departments should be given a greater voice in determining how the plan should be implemented.

Each department should be asked to participate in providing its point of view concerning the plan. Marketing should play a pivotal role in identifying new markets, forecasting likely sales, and selecting the timing of expansion.

Each department manager should evaluate the plan as developed by top management and then advise how the proposed changes will affect his or her department. It's unlikely that a nonaccounting manager will be asked to participate on this level; it's more likely that the plan will be imposed from above, often without consideration for the important nonfinancial issues that will affect you and will ultimately determine whether the plan can succeed or is on an unavoidable course to failure.

How can you influence management to give you a greater voice in the planning process? Below are several steps you can take to change the way the planning process works in your company:

1. Consult with the accounting department. If you are aware of problems involved with next year's business plan, let your accountant know about those problems. Explain them in financial terms, so that your arguments will be valid from the accountant's viewpoint and from the viewpoint of the executive who is concerned with profits.

Example: You are aware that the planned expansion of gross volume will create a transaction burden for your department. You anticipate a requirement for fully automated processing within one year, for training your staff, and for increasing your staff. The budget for these expenses should be communicated to Accounting so that the expansion plan can be methodically planned and financed.

2. Prepare a departmental budget. Use the company's business plan to prepare a budget—not the overall, standard budget you must prepare each year, but a budget just for the proposed growth in the future.

Example: You prepare a departmental budget showing current expense levels next to the expenses you will incur after completion of the new plan. The difference represents the upgrades you will need, in terms of salary expense, new equipment, and training.

3. Submit a report to management. Summarize your departmental budget and submit a report to top management (through the chain of command). Base all of your assumptions on the plan that has already been prepared. Supplement the projected expenses you anticipate, with brief narrative sections explaining why the cost of running your department will rise.

Example: A planning session has been announced for next week. You're aware of the plan's major features, which include expanding the customer base by 50 percent over a six-month period. You write a report that analyzes your department's current transaction load. You assume that a proposed plan will be realized and then describe how that will change your department's mode of operation.

4. Establish and explain goals. Adopt the point of view that the financial and nonfinancial concerns of management are not separate but are aspects of a single plan. Thus, you should establish goals that, while not strictly financial, do pose financial questions. These must be answered by the way you participate in the plan.

Example: You're aware that a plan will mean a much greater workload in your department. One way to express your concern is to point out the problem and then leave it to the accountant and top management to deal with it. A better way to handle the problem is to devise your own goals and present them within the context of a departmental plan.

PLANNING FOR YOUR DEPARTMENT

A companywide plan usually includes a brief company history, description of management and staff, major goals, a marketing plan, assumptions, forecasts and budgets, and financial statements. While this document raises many nonfinancial points, it invariably takes a financial approach. This approach is completely appropriate if we assume the plan exists only for outside venture capitalists and loan sources. But if the plan is to succeed, those nonfinancial issues must be resolved. And that can occur only on the departmental level. This requires that you develop a plan of your own.

Your plan should be developed to address issues of which you are aware, that exist as a ramification of the larger companywide plan. Break your plan into five sections as outlined in Figure 10-1.

1. Premise. Begin your plan by defining your premise. This definition is similar to the assumptions used to build a companywide plan, but organized on a departmental level. The first premise should be that every aspect of the company's plan will go into effect, and by the time specified in the plan. This leads to a question every manager must answer: How will the successful realization of the plan affect my department?

From that point, you will develop a number of other assumptions, all of which lead to your final premise. For example, you may assume that an expansion plan will mean a greater workload, that you will need to hire more people, that existing processing systems will be made obsolete by the plan, or that your department will need more floor space.

The premise should be clearly and briefly stated, and supported by your own detailed analysis. Use historical information, comparing volume to workload or showing how personnel and system capacity will be reached and surpassed.

2. Goals. The second section of your plan should include departmental goals, expressed as positive solutions to the

Figure 10-1.
Departmental plan.

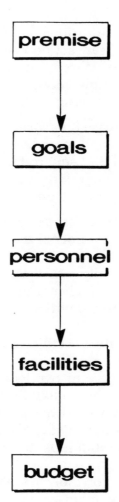

problems you anticipate as the result of the companywide plan.

For example, you expect to need three additional employees and more floor space within the coming year, based on the expressed plan to increase sales volume and the number of customers. One goal should deal with the need for staff expansion and corresponding floor space. Express your goal statements as clearly and as specifically as possible, and always include a tentative deadline. Some examples:

General: To add additional staff members to handle a higher transaction load.

Specific: To hire three additional staff members within eight months, to handle a 40 percent higher transaction load.

General: To increase floor space for the needed staff increases and more file space.

Specific: To add 350 square feet of floor space to the department within six months, for three new employees and additional filing space.

General: To get a better processing system to handle a greater number of transactions in the department.

Specific: To identify the best upgraded system to handle a higher transaction load, within the next three months.

3. Personnel. Devote a section to the issue of your staff. When top management reviews a proposed plan on a companywide basis, it's easy to overlook one reality: Growth also demands more people to handle the work involved. It's easier to believe that the existing staff will be able to handle more work, but that's not always the case. It's your task to demonstrate why your staff must be expanded or to propose other solutions.

If you simply ask for more people, complaining about your overworked department, you cannot expect a supportive and enthusiastic response from top management. Your argument must be based on the facts. And your best facts are those that went into developing the marketing plan management has approved. Identify specific areas where the planned expansion will demand more personnel.

As an alternative to new hires, you can propose that your existing staff members will need to be trained for advanced processing.

Example: You suggest that as an alternative to hiring new people, the current manual system should be replaced with automation. Based on your estimate of the efficiency this would provide, you ask for training instead of new people. Although the initial outlay of capital would be greater, the future expense of running the department would be lower. You demonstrate your ideas with an estimate of future costs.

4. Facilities. Expansion cannot be isolated to gross volume and the bottom line. However, many plans are limited to these factors, ignoring the possible changes in costs and expenses in between. If you create a plan that asks for more space or equipment, be prepared to explain (1) why they're needed and (2) how the resulting efficiency translates to profits.

This section should include systems, floor space, and equipment or machinery. All of these demands will be realistic as long as your analysis is tied to a fair and complete evaluation of how expansion will affect you.

Example: You make a case for hiring two more employees and adding 200 square feet to your department. You base your argument on a one-year business and marketing plan prepared by the accounting department. You point out that the expansion will translate to long-term savings, because of the greater efficiency your staff will have by adding personnel and space. The alternative to this plan is a reduction in quality, inability to ensure meeting report deadlines, and excessive overtime in the department. Your case was well made, because top management realized the need for expansion beyond sales and profits.

5. Budget. Your departmental plan is summarized by a budget which should extend only six months to be realistic. However, if the companywide plan covers an entire year, coordinate your departmental budget request with that period.

The budget is a summary of the issues you presented in other sections. It should be cross-referenced by way of footnotes to the appropriate section of your plan. This strictly financial segment of your report summarizes your case in terms of dollars and cents. To some people's way of thinking, it will be the only important part of the plan, one that can be looked at and endorsed or dismissed. But a budget cannot be reviewed in isolation; the premise and analysis must be reviewed as well.

SETTING DEPARTMENTAL GOALS

A plan must always be based on goals. A goal defines what you hope to achieve, when you want to accomplish the end result, who has responsibility for implementation, what facilities and equipment are needed, and what the required budget is. Each phase of your plan must be considered in the goal. Departmental goals, like those set by top management for the entire company, must be carefully defined in each aspect:

1. The goal statement. A goal must be expressed clearly and in specific language. It's not enough to set the goal that you will "hire more people" to handle an expected growth in workload. That does not define the solution you want to offer, nor does it really define what you need. The goal statement should be clear enough so that anyone who reads it will know exactly what you want to achieve and why.

2. Deadline. A goal is not a goal without a deadline that can be reached. The deadline must match the issue to be considered realistic. If you expect a large increase in transaction volume over the next year, the request for staff increases (or alternatives) must be timed to correspond with the extra workload. Asking for the change before it's needed is wasteful; and delaying it until the crisis is upon you will be expensive and disruptive.

3. Personnel. This phase refers not only to any new people you want to add to your staff, but it must include the assignment of duties to those already in your department or section. Personnel demands should be expressed in terms of a title and the scope of responsibility.

4. Facilities. What additional floor space, files, furniture or equipment will you need in your department? How are these requirements related to the goal you've set? And why are they needed?

Recognizing that floor space and capital assets are investments, you must address the question that is always on top management's mind. Capital and space are finite, and your requests will arrive along with the constant demands from other departments. You will gain approval only if your idea has merit and is essential to the purposes of the companywide plan.

5. Budget. What is the budget for the single goal you've defined? This budget is not to be confused with the annual budget or revision you prepare for the department at large; it concerns only the change resulting from the isolated goal.

Example: You propose upgrading an automated system as an alternative to hiring more staff. You want to add internal memory and two more terminals. The budget for these proposals must include the cost of training (if applicable), as well as the lease or purchase of new equipment and related supplies.

Complete a worksheet similar to the one shown in Figure 10-2 for each goal you develop in your department.

TRACKING YOUR GOALS

Even the thorough development of a goal and its aspects will not ensure that it will be met. Once you know what you hope to achieve, you must follow the progress of that goal. On a companywide basis, a goal for increasing the sales volume or customer base can be followed on a monthly or weekly basis. When results begin falling short of the goal, action can then be taken. But on a departmental basis, the tracking phase is somewhat different.

Your goal must be tracked partially on the basis of actions you can take, and partially on the response you expect from other people. For example, the goal to increase your

Figure 10-2.
Goals worksheet.

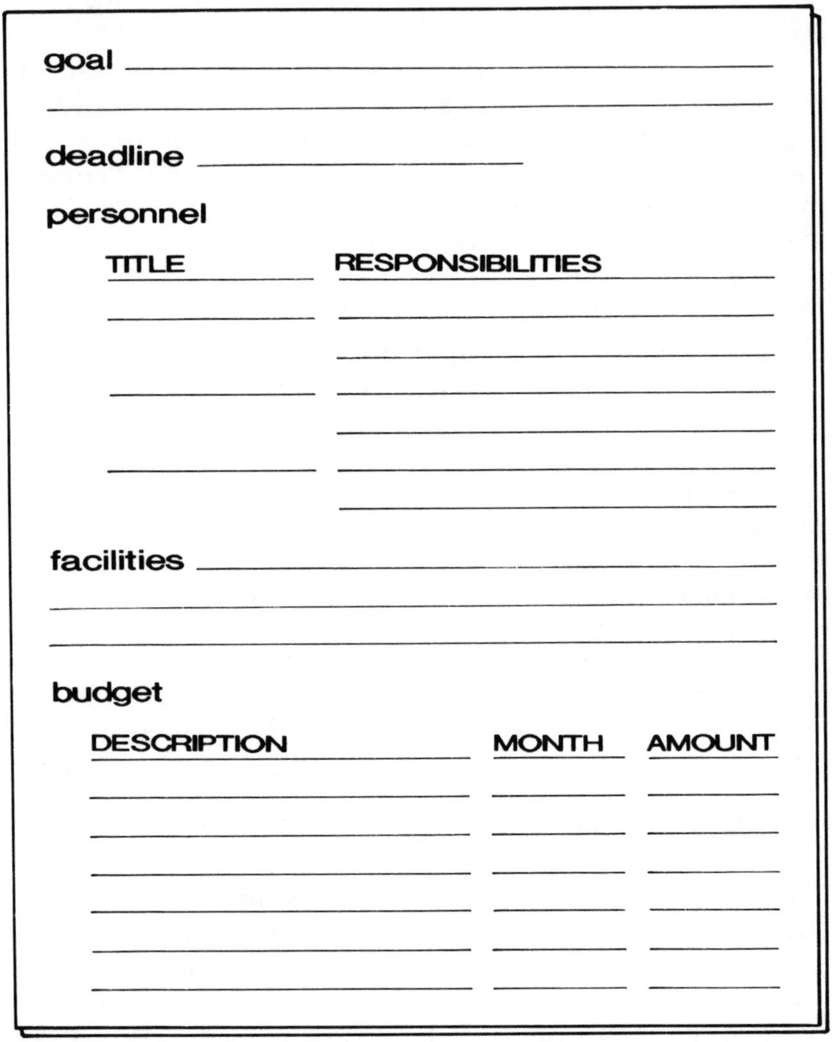

goal _____
_____
deadline _____
personnel

TITLE	RESPONSIBILITIES
_____	_____
	_____
	_____
_____	_____
	_____
_____	_____
	_____

facilities _____

_____

budget

DESCRIPTION	MONTH	AMOUNT
_____	_____	_____
_____	_____	_____
_____	_____	_____
_____	_____	_____
_____	_____	_____
_____	_____	_____

staff over the next few months cannot be completely controlled by a department manager. The manager can take a
limited number of actions:

1. Prepare a report supporting the proposal.
2. Follow up with requests for a decision.
3. Present staffing alternatives.
4. Improve current systems to reduce the need.

Beyond these steps, you must depend on executives or even
on Accounting to formulate a response. Some departmental
goals will depend more on the manager's direct action.

Figure 10-3.
Goal tracking.

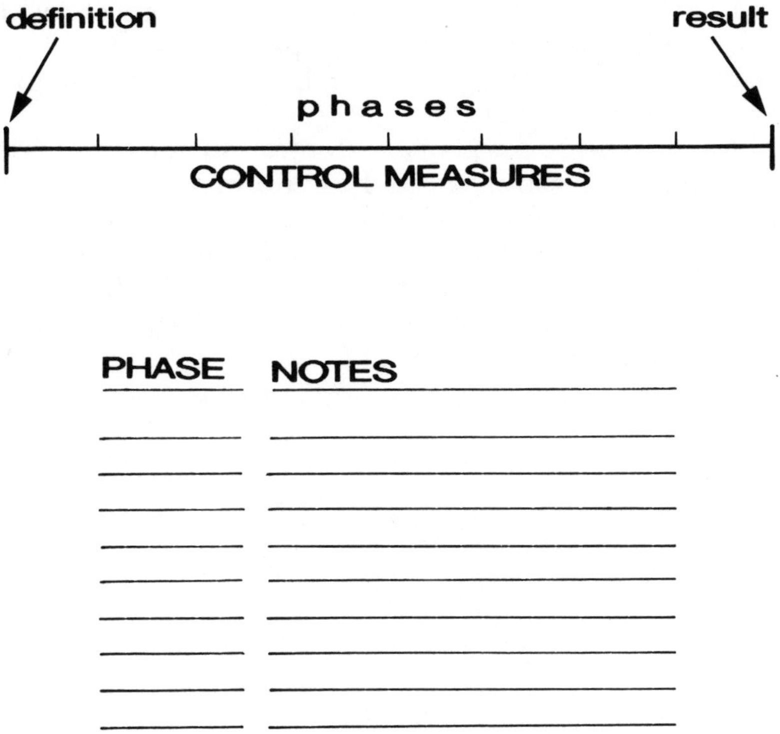

PHASE NOTES

Example: You propose purchasing a new automated system and training your staff in its use, in anticipation of greater volume in the near future. Management approves your request but makes you responsible for training. Over a two-month period, you operate within a goal to fully train everyone in your department. This goal can be accomplished in phases, each one carefully timed and controlled.

In this instance, a tracking and timing line can be used, along with phase steps and notes, as shown in Figure 10-3. The time line begins with definition and ends with the final result. In between, control measures are divided into distinct phases. Thus, even a complex goal can be reduced to manageable segments, each one with its own deadline, and the overall goal is then managed like a project.

Planning on the departmental level is similar to the process on a companywide level. It may be equally as complex, because you must make a series of assumptions about the future. And in some respects, the departmental plan is simplified, especially when its boundaries are defined by a larger companywide plan.

Implementing the plan and controlling it over a period of time requires consistent and careful management. Even with a preliminary worksheet for tracking goals, how do you handle the missed deadline, flawed assumption, or resistance from other departments or individuals? These problems are most often experienced during the budgeting process, discussed in Chapter 11.

Chapter 11

The Purpose of Budgeting

The greatest flaw in most budgeting processes is that the control of that process is given to the accounting department because top management *assumes* that only Accounting can fulfill management's desire for order, uniformity, and responsible reporting. So budgeting takes place under a belief system:

> Myth 1: The accounting department should always prepare budgets for every other department.

If this assumption is examined, its flaw is obvious. How can Accounting calculate the future expenses in your department without knowing anything about your planning priorities, workload, or day-to-day control problems? The answer: It can't.

Management also operates under an assumption that is very harmful to the entire budgeting process:

> Myth 2: Future expenses cannot be accurately estimated or controlled, unless the accounting department tells us how to do it.

Accountants have gained court magician status in many companies because management assumes that all projection exercises employ a scientific method that most of us have not mastered. The truth is, no one can accurately predict future expenses, and the accounting department has no more ESP than the rest of us. This entire belief system leads to the third management assumption:

> Myth 3: The purpose of budgeting is to calcu-
> late, as closely as possible, the future expenses
> of a company and what effect they will have on
> profits.

This assumption is the most misguided of all. Budgeting does not exist to predict the future but to establish a standard. Each department then may operate to create controls that help it achieve a desired result.

You can challenge the general assumptions that subvert the corporation when it comes to budgeting. Since the budget's purpose is to create a situation where everyone operates toward a goal, you may ask these questions:

How can I achieve a goal imposed on me by another department?

What is the purpose of establishing a goal if someone else changes my budget arbitrarily?

What changes must I suggest to management to return the process to its intended purpose?

You can take steps to turn the budgeting process into a valuable management tool, to take back the control you need to achieve the planning responsibility every manager needs, and to help top management begin to view budgeting in an entirely different light.

BUDGETS AS A POLITICAL WEAPON

A common budgeting method calls for Accounting to compile a companywide worksheet, with each department providing the details of its requirements for the coming year. Typically, each manager receives the worksheet in November or early December and is expected to fill in the blanks.

In many companies, management believes it follows a

"participative" budgeting process simply because the accounting department sends blank worksheets to each manager. The truth is, budgeting is not filling in the blanks from January through December. When you do that, you're merely guessing the future but leaving the real decisions to Accounting, where little if anything is known about your goals and problems.

We must make a distinction between three important attributes in budgeting:

1. Responsibility. Who is responsible for budgeting? If the accounting department assumes responsibility, then that department must also be aware of companywide goals for the coming year. Management must believe that Accounting can understand the problems every department faces, devise budgets that address those problems, and contain overall expenses so that profits are maximized.

2. Control. Who will control the budgeting process? If Accounting is in control, then it should also be held responsible for the variances that will arise during the year and for devising the responses required to reverse negative trends.

3. Standards. Who will set budget standards? How will estimates be developed, justified, and reported? How will managers proceed with control actions upon discovery of budget variances? If the accounting department serves as the centralized control point, it should also train other managers how to operate within the process.

A centralized budgeting procedure commonly is at work in the company. In this system, control and standards are assigned to Accounting, but responsibility remains with each department. The obvious inequity of this situation makes the usual budgeting process as *ineffective* as possible. No manager is able to control variances, to take action, or even to create profitable changes in procedures; yet each is expected to explain unfavorable variances that arise during the year.

Thus, a poorly conceived budget is created. Each month's expense levels are assigned arbitrarily, the manager has no voice in expense levels, and the system cannot be changed at the departmental level. But when an unfavorable variance arises, the manager must explain it.

The centralized budgeting process is summarized in Figure 11–1. In this system, Accounting is assumed to be in control; yet when a problem arises, it merely reports, and the manager must explain all variances. To make matters worse, the manager has no way to correct the problem because the control function rests in Accounting.

Controls would be possible if the manager had been allowed to participate in development of the budget. But an unrealistic projection cannot be controlled or made to happen just because top management would like it to be. Many corporations operate with this system in place.

The flaw in centralized budgeting as it is practiced in most cases is that the intended purpose of going through the budgeting process cannot be achieved. The purpose in budgeting should be to:

- Develop a *supportable* assumption about future expense levels.
- Track each month's expense and measure results against the standard represented by the budget.
- Take corrective actions whenever actual expenses vary from the standard.

Power and influence within the company often come down to the identification of the department that controls the budgeting process. If that department or its manager has the power to cut another department's budget without a sound reason, that's a lot of power. And when each budget is developed arbitrarily, the final decision about the budget's level must also be arbitrary.

UNDOING THE POLITICS

Recognizing that budgets mean influence and power, and knowing that "the budget" is used as an excuse to turn down

Figure 11-1.
Centralized budgeting.

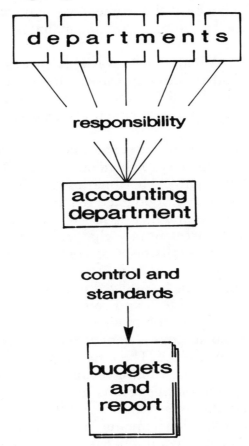

an employee's request, you must know that any change will be threatening to others. You can take steps to change this highly political and illogical procedure without jeopardizing your own position or taking undue risks. To influence management so that change is possible, we must remember the following points:

- No budget has any value unless each department's manager has the power to take action to improve profits and to reduce future expenses.

- A budget is valuable only if problems can be evaluated, which means that every budget must be developed from a base of documented, sound assumptions. Arbitrary budgeting provides management with no value.
- Centralized budgeting invariably means centralized power. And in an organization that depends on specialization by department, any centralization of power must have a detrimental effect on everyone.

Some organizations have experimented with decentralization of budgeting, only to abandon it. The lack of uniform standards, the problem of coordinating deadlines, and varying degrees of quality in budgeted results, all spelled disaster. A badly conceived budgeting procedure was made worse by letting each department take charge.

Decentralization fails because companies do not make a distinction between responsibility, control, and standards. Each department must be allowed to develop its own budget, meaning responsibility and control are assigned at the departmental level. But top management also needs consistent reporting. So standards cannot be decentralized; they must remain in one place. The obvious place for the development, operation, and training of standards is Accounting. Just as accountants compile results from many divisions and create financial statements that are fully documented, the budgets of several departments must be collected and brought together in a comprehensive, well-documented report to top management.

Figure 11–2 illustrates the decentralized budget. Note that each department has responsibility and control for its own individual budget but that the accounting department oversees the process by setting and enforcing standards.

An important point about the decentralized process: The final decision and approval of budgets must not be left to the accounting department. To do so takes the essential control element away from each department and creates a *de facto* centralized system. Accounting can't be ex-

Figure 11-2.
Decentralized budgeting.

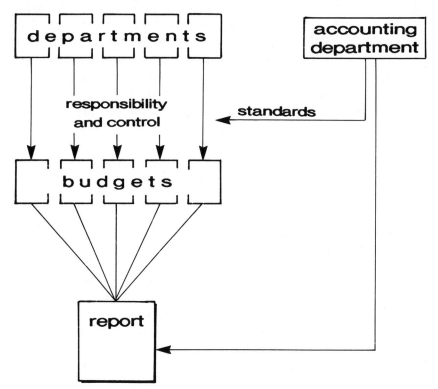

pected to take charge of setting budget levels. Their function should be to produce a well-documented control procedure, through the following means:

- Developing forms and procedure guidelines
- Training department managers in the correct method for completing the budget process
- Reviewing documentation and assumptions, with the purpose of testing for accuracy and support
- Consolidating each department's budget into a companywide document and process
- Reviewing monthly and reporting variances

When the accounting department presents its monthly report to management, variances in each companywide account are identified. In the decentralized system, the variances are traced by department, and each manager is then expected to explain the causes *and* the actions required to correct problems. Here again, attempts at decentralization fail. The accounting department is expected to explain all forms of variance, either with or without consultation to each department. An important point must be raised in this regard:

> If each manager is given the responsibility to develop a budget, then all variances should also be explained by that manager.

Another point concerning variances:

> An unfavorable variance must not be viewed as a problem that must be explained away. Instead, it presents an opportunity to identify a problem and then present a solution to it.

THE CONTROL ISSUE

Improvements in any system will be perceived as a threat to traditional established levels of influence and an unnecessary intrusion. Some will argue that "the time isn't right" or that "our present system works and must not be changed." Recognizing that the real issue is influence, how do you change the balance of control in your company? The best way is to present a plan for change that not only makes sense but points directly and glaringly at the need to create and control future profits. Your plan must emphasize positive change, rather than criticizing the system as it operates today.

Make your suggestion for improving the budgeting process by establishing one premise: Your ideas will lead to increased profits next year. You can demonstrate this by proposing solutions that can be put into effect with the least amount of disruption, effort, or cost. The budgeting process is ideal for this form of change because your ideas will take less time, fewer revisions, and will include built-in mechanisms for control action on the departmental level.

Those who make budget decisions must operate within the guidelines of an assumed profit level. If top management tells the accounting manager to create a budget with a profit higher than the previous year, then budgeting is not a control process but an exercise. Your estimate of next year's expenses is reduced by 30 percent, for example, just because Accounting has been told to produce the desired results.

You may protest the illogic of this method by complaining about it. But that makes you a problem for management, and does not offer a better idea. However, when you offer solutions that simplify the process for everyone, and at the same time improve profits through internal monitoring and control actions, then you have a decent chance of being heard.

ARBITRARY CHANGES

The most frequent complaint managers have about the budgeting process is, "I spent weeks developing a budget for my department, only to have it cut in half." Even when you are given responsibility and control for your own budget, there's always the chance that someone above you in rank will take part of your budget away. Regardless of the reasons for this action, it creates a problem for you during the year, especially if you must answer for unfavorable variances.

How do you report an unfavorable variance when you were not allowed to control your budget? You must refer to your original assumptions and to the imposed change. That's the only way to make the point that arbitrary change leads to variances that cannot be controlled.

Example: You present a budget for office supplies next year based on the assumption that expenses will rise because of an already approved expansion in your staff. Management has also approved a massive revision in your department's record-keeping system, which will require the purchase of several hundreds of dollars in file folders. However, when you present your budget, it comes back with an across-the-board reduction of 30 percent.

You can be sure that unfavorable variances will show up in this account as a result. You must take steps during the budget development phase to revise assumptions so that these variances can be explained intelligently.

Example: When your estimates are reduced by 30 percent, you meet with your supervisor and present your assumptions. Your question: "Which of these assumptions should be reduced to reflect the 30 percent change?"

Obviously, if the reduction was arbitrary, your boss will not have an easy answer to your question. So you are left with two choices: either insist on specific identification, or plan to address variances with the arbitrary changes in mind. Neither alternative completely solves the problem, which is that the change has been made without respect for the intended purpose of the budget. Such changes subvert the entire effort and make budgeting an exercise in frustration, rather than a means for controlling future expenses and reaching profit goals.

How can arbitrary changes be explained in a budget variance report?

Example: You prepare a budget for office supply expenses and your immediate supervisor reduces each month's total by 30 percent. At the end of the first quarter, your department shows an unfavorable variance of 22 percent.

If reductions had not been imposed on your budget, the actual expenses would be running below your original estimate and the variance would not be an issue. However, you now must explain why the variance has occurred (that is, you must take responsibility for the apparent failure in your budget). At the same time, discretion prevents you from pointing the finger at your boss and saying, "It's his fault, not mine."

The solution: Your variance explanation must be presented not only on the basis of the final (arbitrary) budget, but on the basis of your original assumptions *as adjusted* by someone else. Thus, the line-by-line detail of your budget is compared to what constitutes the actual expenses in the account; add to that the variances created by the arbitrary change. Thus, a 30 percent reduction in each month's budget accumulates as one of the factors making up the variance.

This procedure does not point the finger at anyone. It only establishes the fact that even a well-documented series of assumptions can be affected by arbitrary change. The important element here is that a review of the account reveals the source of variance. And the major contributor is the arbitrary reduction.

THE ASSUMPTION BASE

Assumptions can be developed in a number of ways. One common method is to begin with the previous year's budget, add 10 percent, and divide the total by 12. The result is the monthly budget. This simple process is one of the most troublesome. In the event of a variance, what was the cause? It is not adequate to merely state that the budget did not anticipate the actual level of expense or to assume that a variance was created by a "timing difference" that will be absorbed in later months. An intelligent analysis depends on intelligent assumptions at the very beginning of the process.

Every account's budget must be developed on the most logical assumption base, which may not be the same for every account. Sources for building your budget assumptions, summarized in Figure 11-3, include:

1. Historical information. If you are aware of the trend in the recent past, you can estimate the range of likely expense levels in the future. This method provides you with a

Figure 11-3.
Assumption sources.

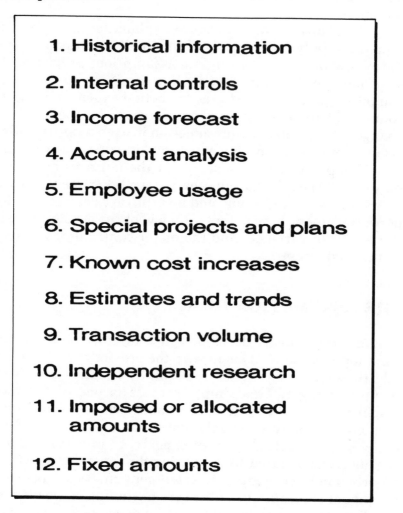

1. Historical information

2. Internal controls

3. Income forecast

4. Account analysis

5. Employee usage

6. Special projects and plans

7. Known cost increases

8. Estimates and trends

9. Transaction volume

10. Independent research

11. Imposed or allocated
    amounts

12. Fixed amounts

guideline for checking how reasonably your budget levels compare with the past.

2. Internal controls. Historical information should be thought of as a starting point, not the last word for creating an estimate. Developing ideas for internal controls over spending will help reduce historical levels and can also serve as your assumption for a future budget level.

3. Income forecast. Many expenses will vary directly or indirectly, as the result of income levels. With this significant fact in mind, your budget can be prepared in a more informed way if the income forecast has already been completed.

4. Account analysis. Studying the types of transactions that occurred in an account for the past year may provide clues and clarification in constructing a new budget, especially in high-volume accounts, such as office supplies.

5. Employee use. Many accounts are most logically analyzed on the basis of employee use, or the expense per employee. One example is office supplies: In certain departments, telephone and photocopying expenses will also vary by employee.

6. Special projects and plans. If your organization has announced a new marketing plan in which products, services, or territories are to be expanded, determine whether that plan will have an impact on your budget. Adjust your assumptions accordingly.

7. Known cost increases. If major suppliers have announced pending cost increases, those increases should be built into your budget. Utility companies, the postal service, and even your local vendors may preannounce rate hikes and across-the-board price increases many months in advance.

8. Estimates and trends. This budgeting procedure is the least dependable and the most common. Estimates and trends are appropriate in some instances. When a level of expense simply cannot be scientifically known in advance, an estimate must suffice.

9. Transaction volume. Departments involved strictly in processing can estimate many expenses on the number of units to be handled, including salary expenses. The "units" approach is used in cost accounting in a manufacturing environment; the same idea can be applied to any department that handles transactions.

10. Independent research. You are not restricted to information handed to you or available in your own files. Make calls, get information from other departments and even from sources outside your own company.

11. Imposed or allocated amounts. Your accounting department might arbitrarily assign expenses without consulting you. When you run into an unfavorable variance in an account with an arbitrary or imposed budget, always refer to the source.

12. Fixed amounts. Refer to a contract or permanent arrangement when an expense budget is fixed.

A SIMPLE APPROACH

Budgets end up as time-consuming exercises because the development phase occurs in chaos. You must start with a series of intelligent assumptions. If your assumptions are correct, the number of revisions will be reduced, the chances for someone else to change your budget are eliminated, and your records support the month-to-month work necessary to explain variances.

Accountants are trained to be prepared to prove everything they report. So they develop worksheets showing calculations, they write down sources of information, and they verify facts on their own.

You will simplify your budgeting task by concentrating on the intelligent development of assumptions as a first step. Only then are your numbers developed for presentation to management.

Figure 11-4 shows a sample of a budget assumptions worksheet. This worksheet identifies the account, your department, the date prepared, and the budget year. Then each month's budget is shown on its own line, with room for up to four components.

A *component* is a contributing factor to your budget. For example, under your office supplies account, you might find it useful to break your budget down by major supplier, by type of expense, or by recurring versus nonrecurring supplies. Telephone expenses can be divided between fixed

Figure 11-4.
Budget assumption worksheet.

Budget Assumption Worksheet

Account _____

Department _____

Date prepared _____ year _____

MONTH	1	2	3	4	TOTAL
Jan					
Feb					
Mar					
Apr					
May					
Jun					
Jul					
Aug					
Sep					
Oct					
Nov					
Dec					
Total					

EXPLANATION

1. _____
   _____

Assumption method: _____

2. _____
   _____

Assumption method: _____

3. _____
   _____

Assumption method: _____

4. _____
   _____

Assumption method: _____

monthly charges or allocations, local calls, long-distance domestic calls, and international calls. Showing the components will help you to explain your budget variances throughout the year. Comparisons can then be made in the same breakdown as your budget so that the causes of variances can be isolated and explained.

The assumption worksheet must also include a brief explanation of each component. Thus, a reviewer will be able to understand what makes up the budget for a single account in your department. The explanation should include your assumption method (historical information, estimates and trends, or fixed amounts, for example).

This breakdown also helps you to defend against arbitrary change. Without it, you have no argument to prevent a change from occurring. With it, you can properly question the reasons for a change.

THE CORRECT CONTROL MECHANISM

Don't fall into the trap of thinking of the budget as a series of columns and rows of numbers. That's just the final document that should support a process of setting goals, planning profits, and building a method for controlling cash flow in the near future.

The mechanism of budgeting should involve a series of logical steps, summarized in Figure 11-5, all aimed at achieving the intended purpose:

1. Assumptions. Begin developing budgets with a series of logical assumptions that might include the method of estimating, as well as the breakdown of the account into its components.

2. Documentation. Write down everything you do in the process of building assumptions. Explain the method used to arrive at estimates.

3. Test and review. Before submitting your preliminary budget, review totals, check assumptions and results, and make necessary changes.

Figure 11-5.
The budget and control process.

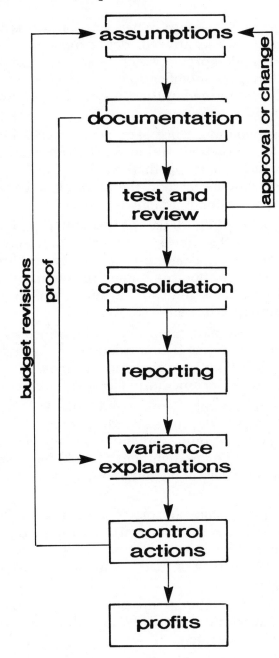

4. Approval or change. When your budget is presented to the committee, executive, or department that makes the final decision and approval, you may receive changes. These changes will require modification to your assumptions, or in the case of unsupported and arbitrary change, notation on your assumption worksheet.

5. Consolidation. Once each department's budget has been completed, revised, and approved, the budget for the whole company is put together. At this phase, the departmental preparation ends and the accounting department's analysis and reporting functions take over.

6. Reporting. Completion of the annual budget is only the beginning of the process. The important and valuable work must occur on a month-to-month basis, through the reporting system. A monthly budget review meeting is held to study reasons for significant variances and to determine corrective actions required.

7. Variance explanations. The explanations you develop can be extremely difficult if you have not documented the detailed assumptions of your budget; they can be quite simple if you have documentation as reference material.

8. Control actions. Controls may take the form of procedures aimed at curtailing a spending trend, installation of automated systems, improvements over internal operating procedures, hiring or realignment of staff and responsibilities, or upon discovery of budget flaws, a revision of the budget itself.

9. Budget revisions. In some companies, semiannual or even quarterly budget revisions are the accepted procedure. Because the process is so time-consuming, some managers are constantly working on budgets at some phase of preparation or approval.

10. Profits. If the budgeting process has been employed in its intended manner, the company will be able to predict and control future profits.

If used as it should be, your budget can serve as a management tool. Avoid the power struggles and influences that make budgeting a negative. Suggest positive and constructive changes, not only in the way that budget responsibility and control are assigned, but also in:

- Revision procedures and frequency
- Variance reporting
- Control actions

Chapter 12 explains how to convert budgets into useful management tools for controlling future profits and how to reduce the time-consuming and bureaucratic attributes of budgeting.

Chapter 12

Budgets as a Management Tool

Once a budget has been finalized, the job has just begun. An approved budget is merely definition. It documents standards the company has set for itself, goals it wants to reach, and the means for periodic monitoring. The consolidated budget is the estimated result management wants for the entire company. Departmental budgets are each manager's individual control standard.

For these standards to be met, you must be able to track and compare expenses to the budget, look for variances, and take action to keep expenses in line. Or, when the budget is flawed, you must be able to revise it so that the *standard* is realistic.

WHEN THE BUDGET IS DONE

An important point to keep in mind is:

> The whole budgeting process is useful only when it is used to indicate actions that must be taken to correct problems.

The implications of this idea point to the flaw in a highly bureaucratic system where budgets are created and then left in a desk drawer. What is the purpose in taking on the huge task of putting together the budget if no action will be taken later? Upon discovery of a negative trend, you must act;

otherwise, you might as well eliminate the budgeting process.

This sensible, basic truth should be observed in setting the budgeting rule for every organization. Unfortunately, getting top management to enforce the idea might not be an easy task. To many people, completing the definition phase of budgeting is perceived as the primary task. Spending time to later discover problems is a lower priority and does not lead to action.

A second important point to remember about budgeting is:

> When you know a budget is unrealistic, it no longer serves a useful purpose but must be revised.

Recognizing that the creation of a budget takes a great deal of staff and executive time, most organizations limit the process to one yearly budget and a six-month revision. This system demands that a company live with an obviously flawed budget for at least half the year, in spite of how little value it provides.

The alternative is to establish standards for the budgeting process. First, a budget can only be of practical use for a six-month period. Thus, rather than conforming to the traditional full-year budget, it makes more sense to budget for half-year intervals. This format reduces the scope of the task and still provides you with a standard. Management is oriented toward full-year estimating of future revenues and expenses because the fiscal year is the standard unit for reporting the past. In other words, the future, as hard as it is to predict, is forced to conform to the format of the past.

Second, view budget preparation in a realistic manner. Budgeting causes great pressure because managers believe they are expected to accurately predict the future. In fact, though, your real purpose in budgeting is to set goals and to then do all in your power to reach those goals. In the case of expenses, your goal is to not exceed a reasonable and realistic level of expense.

Third, simplify the initial process of budget preparation. Rather than wasting time with endless reviews, arbitrary changes, and poorly documented guesses, a carefully constructed series of assumptions should serve as the basis for a six-month budget.

You will find it extremely difficult to change the way your company prepares and acts on its budgets. The best you can expect is to have a hearing of your ideas and suggestions. Changes, if any, will be gradual, based on the logic and simplicity of what you propose. If you can demonstrate how budgets can be changed from highly political exercises to processes for creating profits, then top management will eventually respond.

THE BEGINNING OF YOUR JOB

Typically, you are expected to spend two to three weeks in the last month of the year filling out worksheets and meeting with a budget committee to formulate your department's budget. As satisfying as it is to finish this phase of the task, your job is just beginning.

From that point forward, the budget can be put to work as your monitoring device for expenses. Your goal (budget) is the standard for measuring and controlling actual expense levels. That's the perfect application of the budget. But in practice, this application often is prevented.

A budget is of no practical value when top management has a preconceived idea of what it wants to achieve in the coming year—or at least, what it intends to promise the chairman, the president, or the stockholders. Your company's management is probably under considerable pressure to exceed last year's profit level, to produce greater volume, to improve cash flow, and to hold expenses down while expanding at an accelerated rate.

In response to these pressures, management imposes minimum budgeting results, before any analysis begins. For example, you might be told that expenses must remain at last year's level, or even be reduced. At the same time, the forecast of future income is increased by 10, 20, or 30 percent. And if the collective budgets for each department do not yield the profit expectation, then expense estimates will be cut.

A more realistic approach would be for management to set a different standard: that profitable volume must be increased by a realistic percentage (based on market share, competition, and capital restrictions). The budget should be prepared based on sales forecasts and not on some arbitrary formula compared to the previous year. Any growth in profits is then derived from the careful control over increases in overhead. The margin of profit can be increased by holding down fixed overhead during expansion periods. That's where a logical and controlled budgetary process is best applied.

As an important corollary of this approach, budgets for variable expenses (those expenses that will change based on sales activity) must be prepared based on changes in income forecasts. In most companies, the forecast is completed last or as a completely separate function from expense budgets. Every manager knows that income levels dictate the degree of expense, that expense varies based on the support level for income generated, and that certain expenses must be budgeted with changes in volume.

If your company does not hold monthly budget review meetings, you should recommend that it does. These meetings should be brief and should lead to specific actions to correct negative variances. If your company does hold variance review meetings, ask yourself these questions:

Are variance explanations worthwhile? That is, do the explanations indicate actions that should be taken now to correct a problem?

Are variances identified by department or responsibility, or are they reported companywide, in more general terms?

Are follow-up, corrective actions assigned and reviewed the next month?

VARIANCE REPORTING

Reporting on minor variances is not an economic use of time, so a standard must be set to identify a significant variance. The standard should isolate variances in terms of amount and percentage above or below budget. Both favorable and unfavorable variances should be explained.

Why explain a favorable variance? The budget is intended as a fair estimate of what should be spent during the year. If actual expenses are below budget, a problem is indicated. For example, the budget might have been prepared with too much padding, which affects management's ability to plan and set standards. Or the timing of an expense might be off by a month or two. Thus, the causes of favorable variances should be identified.

Establishing a fair standard depends on the amount of money in the budget, the relationship between expenses and sales volume, and the amount of net profit your company realizes monthly and annually. For example, in an organization that reports sales in the hundreds of millions, and monthly profits in hundreds of thousands, a $1,000 variance might be seen as insignificant. But in a company with only $1 million in sales and profits of less than $50,000 per year, a $300 variance could be a very significant problem.

Relatively small variances in a number of different accounts can add up to an overall large problem for your company. Keep this idea in mind when identifying what constitutes "significant" variances. As a rule of thumb, your definition of a significant variance should allow for explanations of three-fourths or more of the total amount of expense variance each month. Define a significant variance by combining percentage and amount. For example:

> A variance is significant and must be explained when the amount of variance is more than $100 and is more than 10 percent of the year-to-date budget.
> A variance is significant and must be explained when the amount of variance is more than $500 and is more than 5 percent of the year-to-date budget.

Budgets may be reported on a monthly or year-to-date basis. One advantage of the monthly format is that it allows you to report on the current problems only, without regard for year-to-date problems that have already occurred and been explained (and hopefully, acted upon). Another advantage is that it overcomes the absorption problem. Unfavorable variances in one month are often absorbed by overbudgeted allowances in the following month.

Year-to-date reporting, however, might be more practical for a number of reasons. Budgets are only estimates, and month-to-month variances often are properly absorbed. The exact timing of an expenditure cannot be easily pinned down when a budget is prepared, and year-to-date reporting tends to offset that problem. Once a current problem is identified, a subsequent month's explanation can easily isolate and explain a problem by describing (1) previously discovered variances and (2) new problems.

THE VARIANCE REPORT

The monthly budget review meeting should be short and should involve each department manager who participated in the budget process. If the review committee consists of the president, the treasurer, and the accountant, then review will take place in a vacuum. As long as each manager is to be held responsible for budget preparation, each manager should be involved in budget review.

You can respond to criticism of your budget only when you're given the chance to explain how and why a variance has occurred. And if you are not consulted when explanations are written, then the entire review process is a waste of time. An even more important reason to include every department manager in this process is:

> If any action is to be taken to correct a discovered problem, it must be assigned to the manager of the department in which the problem exists.

Accountants view budgeting as more difficult when they are given misplaced responsibility. They must determine the causes of variances and explain to management why a problem exists. In most cases, there is no indication for corrective action. The problem is identified and left at that. If the accountant does approach you to discuss the problem, you are unlikely to respond with enthusiasm. And why should you, when you are left out of the review process and approached only when a problem comes up? So accountants may think of you as uncooperative and apathetic, an understandable attitude when budgets are misused.

A variance report should be as simple as possible. In highly decentralized companies, it might be worthwhile to prepare a report for each department. But in most organizations, management is concerned with an overview. So the report will be in efficient, consolidated form, since the explanation will identify departmental causes for a companywide problem.

The report should list each expense in the same sequence that it is reported on the income statement. The actual year-to-date expense total is listed, followed by the year-to-date budget. A column should be added for cross-reference to explanations, which appear on the next page. Finally, the variance amount and percentage are shown. The note, variance amount, and variance percentage columns should be filled in only for those accounts with significant variances. Figure 12-1 shows a sample form.

An example of how variances would be expressed: At the end of May, the year-to-date actual and budget totals are compared. In this case, a "significant" variance is defined as one that exceeds $100 of budget, and is off by 10 percent or more. The results for several accounts are:

Variance Worksheet

Description	Actual	Budget	Note	Variance	%
Office Supplies	$4,718	$3,700	1	(1,018)	28
Printing	2,993	2,800			

Variance Worksheet

Description	Actual	Budget	Note	Variance	%
Postage	1,011	900	2	(111)	12
Insurance	8,236	9,000			

In this example, only two accounts require explanation. Both office supply and postage variances meet the criteria of $100 and 10 percent. Even though the printing account's variance is higher than the postage variance, it is not "significant" by the definition in use.

The note column refers to an explanation, which ap-

Figure 12-1.
Variance report.

Variance Report				
Month _____ Year _____				

DESCRIPTION	ACTUAL	BUDGET	NOTE	VARIANCE	%
	$ _____	$ _____		$ _____	___%

pears on the following page of the report. Isolating the financial summary and narrative sections is a good idea because it allows an executive to review the full picture without being distracted by details and review explanations.

Each variance explanation should be summarized on a worksheet that includes the account name, variance amount, and explanation, a sample of which is shown in Figure 12-2. Each month's report may require several pages, depending on the number of variances being reported.

The only way that an explanation can have any meaning is if it is tied to the original assumptions used to create the budget. Otherwise, no one can possibly know where the problem came from or how to correct it.

Examples of poorly written explanations:

The variance exists because actual expenses exceeded budget by 12 percent.

This unfavorable variance is expected to be absorbed in coming months.

Expense levels were greater than anticipated at the time the budget was prepared.

Anyone who has participated in variance review will recognize these explanations as typical, but none even come close to explaining the reasons for a variance. The first merely restates the degree of variance, in narrative form. The second admits that a budgeting problem exists, but expresses the hope that future months were overbudgeted enough to offset the problem. And the third is an obvious version of the problem, without any definition.

MEANINGFUL EXPLANATIONS

Managers given the task of writing explanations of unfavorable variances face a difficult task, especially when they re-

Figure 12-2.
Variance worksheet.

Variance Worksheet

Month _____ Year _____

ACCOUNT	VARIANCE	EXPLANATION
_____	$ _____	_____
		_____
		_____
_____	_____	_____
		_____
		_____
_____	_____	_____
		_____
		_____
_____	_____	_____
		_____
		_____
_____	_____	_____
		_____
		_____
_____	_____	_____
		_____
		_____
_____	_____	_____
		_____
		_____
_____	_____	_____
		_____

---

alize that a budget is flawed, expenses were underestimated, and that there probably is no easy cure for the problem. The job is made even harder when a budget is prepared without a base of sound assumptions. In that case, you cannot truly know why the variance exists because no control mechanisms or standards exist.

However, there are a limited number of acceptable variances, and these could be explained by one or more of the following:

Inadequate budget. Among the most difficult variances to explain is one that develops because the budget was not prepared well. If you did the original budget but did not foresee a significant expense, you will have to admit your error. Two suggestions: First, state this fact clearly and honestly, without trying to hedge words or look for other reasons. And second, make a note of the error and place that note in your file for the next budget. You can learn from mistakes and improve your budgeting abilities in subsequent periods.

Arbitrary change. Variances are also difficult to explain when your well-constructed original budget is reduced by someone else. In this case, reconcile the actual expense level to your original assumptions, and then identify the variance amount due to the reduction.

Unexpected expense. You cannot possibly anticipate every expense that will be coded to a particular account. When an expense comes up that is not in your budget, use that as your reason for the variance. And again, make a note for next year's file.

Lack of internal control. When variance occurs in expense accounts that require management and systems for monitoring expense levels, you should point out where controls are lacking. For example, office supplies might be better controlled with centralized purchasing and a requisition system. Telephone expenses can be recorded on a phone log, and monthly bills reconciled and checked. And multidepartmental use of a single photocopy machine should be expensed out by allocation, based on user keys or written vouchers.

Allocation. Part of your current expense might consist of expenses allocated to each department. If those allocations are not included in your original assumptions and budget, they should be identified as the cause of an unfavorable variance.

Timing of expenses. Some expenses are budgeted in one month, but will not be booked until the following month or booked before the month budgeted. In those cases, cite timing as the cause. But a word of caution: Use this explanation *only* when you're certain that it is the cause. This explanation often is used when the manager cannot identify the real problem.

Coding error. In analyzing the contents of an account, you might discover that a certain transaction has been posted to the wrong account, causing variances in two accounts—the one you are studying, and the one that it belongs in. Identify the problem and ensure that a correcting journal entry is prepared.

Vendor price changes. Inflation will affect your budget but cannot always be anticipated. If your assumptions did not allow for price increases, but vendors are now charging higher rates, include this in your explanation.

Variance explanations are summarized in Figure 12-3.

A single explanation could consist of two or more causes, in which case it should be broken down and summarized. The more complete and precise your explanation, the more useful it will be in determining appropriate action and assigning it to the right person.

Every explanation should include an obvious corrective action or should spell out what you recommend. This idea will be considered an innovative and drastic departure from tradition in most companies, but it makes sense, considering the purpose of budget review.

THE REVISION PROBLEM

Any budget review will invariably date the budget itself. The greater the time involved, the less accurate your existing budget and the greater the need for revision.

In organizations that devote considerable time to the preparation phase of budgeting, it seems that the process never ends. Just as you complete one final budget for the year, it's time to prepare a revision. In some companies, a

Figure 12-3.
Variance explanations.

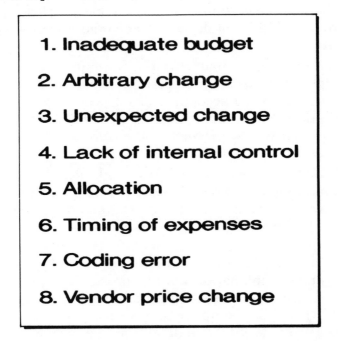

1. Inadequate budget

2. Arbitrary change

3. Unexpected change

4. Lack of internal control

5. Allocation

6. Timing of expenses

7. Coding error

8. Vendor price change

full-blown revision process might be called for at the end of each quarter. That means that every department manager must waste many weeks to prepare revised budgets, sit in endless meetings, fill out worksheets, and take time away from more productive tasks.

This problem would be eliminated if companies would abandon the assumed need for a twelve-month budget. Revisions are necessary because of a misguided belief that estimates must be accurate. That's simply not realistic. Some points to raise in support of a six-month budget:

Change is constant. Management's programs and objectives change over time, in response to a dynamic market, new products and competition, and discovered expansion opportunities, invariably making an existing year-long budget obsolete.

Revisions can be misused. Revisions often subvert the identification and control of unfavorable variances. Rather than defining a problem and then taking action, it's often easier to wait for an upcoming revision and bury the problem in a larger budget.

Full-year budgets take more time. The twelve-month budgeting process demands a great deal of time, because energy is put into estimating expenses a full year away, even with full knowledge that the operating and marketing environment will change drastically before that time arrives.

Six-month review is easier. A six-month budget provides the means for immediate review, with a greater likelihood that the causes of variance will be identified and corrective action taken.

As an alternative to the traditional twelve-month budget with a six-month revision, consider this procedure:

- Each budget will be prepared for a six-month period, and no overall revisions will be allowed during that time.
- In the preparatory phase, each department will, under guidelines controlled by the accounting department, compile its own budget and document assumptions.
- The accounting department will be responsible for consolidating departmental expense budgets and will work directly with sales and marketing management in developing revenue forecasts and direct cost budgets.
- Accounting will also prepare six-month cash flow projections.

As part of this simplified and practical approach, it should be possible to revise the budget for an isolated account, but *only* upon discovery of a major flaw. When you find that your assumptions are flawed, that account's budget is rendered obsolete. Thus, it makes no sense to continue using it as a standard for internal control.

This suggestion could lead to greater bureaucracy and paperwork if the volume of revisions is allowed to get out of

Figure 12-4.
Revision worksheet.

Revision Worksheet

Date _____

Account _____ Department _____

Variance $ _____   through ___/___/___

Cause of variance _____
_____
_____
_____

(Attach revised budget assumption worksheet)

PROPOSED REVISION

MONTH	ORIGINAL BUDGET	CHANGE	REVISED BUDGET
	$	$	$
TOTAL	$	$	$

hand. So suggested revisions must be carefully controlled and reviewed and only approved in the most extreme cases.

A revision worksheet should be prepared by the manager recommending the revision. While increasing the volume of forms involved in the budgeting process is contrary to your goal of simplification, this form is necessary. Only by reviewing your proposal in writing can management determine whether the problem justifies a revision.

Figure 12-4 shows a sample of a revision worksheet. It includes identification of the account, department, amount of variance, and the period involved. The cause of the variance is written out, followed by a summary of the original budget, suggested revision, and revised budget. Note that only six spaces are allowed for this, in line with the proposed limited-period budget.

Even a moderately high volume of departmental budget revisions can be handled easily if Accounting maintains the consolidated budget with an automated spreadsheet program. A great volume of departmental breakdown and consolidated versions of a budget, even with several changes during the six months, can thus be easily documented and controlled.

If an automated spreadsheet program is not in use, all changes in the budget must be carefully documented and controlled by cross-reference. Otherwise, it becomes a hopelessly disorganized mess that no one can track. The accounting department should establish a procedure for controlling all such changes, which is exactly the type of audit trail to which they are accustomed.

A well-designed and controlled budget leads naturally to the types of controls the process is intended to provide. Chapter 13 shows how profitable control measures are generated from a properly managed budgeting procedure and how those ideas can be implemented in your department.

Chapter 13

Controls and
Your Budget

Chapter 12 described the budget as a means for identifying problems needing correction. The exercise of estimating the future is worthwhile only if the process includes this review and only if you are able to use the information to take action.

REDEFINING BUDGETARY RESPONSIBILITIES

As an alternative to the review of budgets by committee or one central department, each department manager should be allowed to (1) originate the budget in the first place, (2) participate in the study of variances and trends, and (3) assume responsibility for follow-up action. The entire process may certainly be controlled centrally, and the accounting department should be used for this purpose. However, when a particular expense is running over budget in *your* department, how can someone else control it? And what direct controls can they enforce?

Top management does not easily accept the idea of decentralized budget review and action. It means that more people must be involved in the reporting chain, and the simple efficiency of centralized reporting appears to make more sense. However, that more common approach is not logical; the reporting department or committee cannot be made responsible for fixing the problem.

Inviting every department manager to a monthly budget reporting and review meeting probably is impractical. The problems created by a large meeting will counteract any benefits of departmental responsibility. Some solutions you can suggest for minimizing the problems arising from every department's participation:

- Accounting should function as a centralized control point that coordinates standards for all phases of budgeting and reporting.
- Accounting presents the companywide budget variance report, with variance explanations given by department or gathered by Accounting and then summarized as part of its report.
- Each department provides its own variance explanations to Accounting and also to a divisional or section executive.
- The executive (control person) represents a group of departments at the budget review meeting.

Figure 13-1 shows this proposed reporting structure.

A number of departments are represented by one control person. The accounting department provides standards so that reporting is consistent and appropriate to the task. Then Accounting and each control person attend the monthly budget review meeting.

Whether each manager attends the budget review meeting, or is represented by a vice-president or other control person, this procedure allows you and other department managers to accept responsibility for variances within your control. Thus, corrective actions are possible. A key point:

> As long as management insists that each manager take action to correct negative trends, the budgeting process works well.

This idea is interesting in theory alone, if the responsible manager is not expected to take corrective action. Whenever a negative variance is discovered, it must be dealt with by the following steps:

Figure 13-1.
Budgeting report chart.

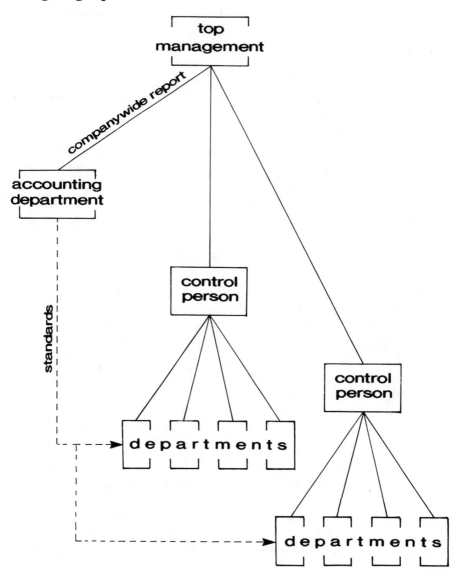

1. It must be explained in reference to the budget assumptions.
2. The responsible manager must be allowed (and expected) to take action to reverse a negative trend.
3. The accounting department advises each department on possible corrective actions.

The importance of using budget assumptions as the basis for explanation was discussed in Chapter 12. Steps 2 and 3, however, present greater difficulty in implementing this idea.

Simply stating that a particular department manager must be held responsible for taking action is not enough. Top management must ensure that the idea filters down through the ranks, and that managers are allowed to follow up with expense controls. In addition, the individuals in the middle of the chain of command must be expected to ensure that each manager does, in fact, take the actions that are mandated by budget discoveries.

These requirements might represent major changes in the way your company operates. Accountability and follow-through are never easily put into effect, especially when that means changing the way things have been done (or not done) in the past. The only way to enforce the new idea is with patient explanation and internal education. We must also assume that top management endorses and fully supports this system. Remember:

> A new idea can work only when your company's leadership believes in it, and insists that it be put into action.

You bring up a sensitive issue whenever you suggest any major form of change, especially when that change involves reducing another department's responsibility, influence, and power. If Accounting is currently in charge of budget reporting, suggesting that it should act in an advisory role could lead to strong resistance.

The accounting department plays two crucial roles in

the revised budget reporting chain. First, it advises each department and enforces uniform reporting standards. Second, it presents the consolidated report to management.

To overcome the resistance to a suggested change, the emphasis should be put on responsibility and not on power or influence issues. To suggest that budget reporting should be "taken away" from Accounting doesn't describe the new procedure. That report must continue. However, responsibility for explaining and then following up on discovered negative trends rests with each department. Accounting works in the reporting role, identifying sources and responsibility for the variances, and ensuring that follow-up occurs.

There is no shift in power and influence; a reporting and coordinating role belongs to the accounting department. The revision will not take away from Accounting's role; it only removes an unreasonable form of pressure from it—to account for variances beyond its control.

SPOTTING TRENDS

Let's assume that you propose a complete revision to your budgeting process, management endorses the idea and puts it into effect, and the accounting department happily accepts its redefined role. You must still be able to spot emerging trends and catch the negatives before they eat away at profits.

You must expect change to occur slowly. And as difficult as it might seem to get to this point, the change is essential if budgeting is to contain any validity. You must operate with several assumptions: First, that management will accept your suggestion for the change. Second, that the various executives and managers in the chain of command will actively participate in the way they should. Third, that the accounting department will play the critical redefined role. And fourth, that you will be able to spot trends in your department and correct them.

All of these changes represent a complete reevaluation

of the management role and, in many cases, a precise identification of responsibility. The corporate culture might
rebel against such specific definitions, especially if a bureaucratic system has allowed inactive reporting procedures to
become the norm. But keep this point in mind when you suggest revising the budget philosophy in your company:

> Sound, realistic budgeting is the cornerstone of
> responsible management, and creating change
> to reach financial goals is the essence of every
> manager's job.

In executing the responsibility for spotting trends, you
must consider the nature of the account, what standards
must be applied to test expense levels, and how the current
trend's significance can be given meaning.

Example: Office supplies were always budgeted in your department based on the previous year's expense levels. This system is now
considered unacceptable, since it builds in overspending as a permanent feature of the budget. You institute a different budgeting
method, based on the average office supply cost per employee. During
the year, you track expense trends by comparing each month's expense
to the number of employees in your department.

This procedure requires some adjustments. For example,
one month's expense includes purchase of a full-year supply
of file folders. If that purchase is included in the month's
total, it will distort the trend, so that expense is removed
from your monthly total.

A six-month trend analysis is shown in Figure 13-2. In
this example, the office supply expense account is related to
the number of employees, so a ratio is developed for the
analysis. The expense total is divided by the number of employees, and the ratio is reported as a dollar amount, representing expenses per employee.

In this example, the monthly expense gradually increases throughout the year. Your task, upon review, is to de-

Figure 13-2.
Ratio analysis.

MONTH	OFFICE SUPPLIES	STAFF	RATIO
Jan	$1,493	37	$40.35
Feb	1,619	39	41.51
Mar	1,643	39	42.13
Apr	1,622	38	42.68
May	1,651	39	42.33
Jun	1,664	39	42.67

termine whether the trend will continue and what that
means. Have you budgeted for these increases, based on vendor price changes? What standard did you use when building your budget assumption base? And what can you do to
reduce the per-employee expense?

If you examine your original assumptions and conclude
that a negative trend is under way, you will have to decide
what actions to take. For example, you look back at the assumption worksheet you prepared at the beginning of the
year. Office supplies were budgeted at $40 per employee. The
number of employees is correct, based on your assumptions
for monthly expenses. But the amount of expense is running
above your goal.

In many companies, this level of discovery would be
considered exceptional. Thus, a variance explanation for the
month of June might read:

> Office supply expenses were budgeted to average $40 per
> employee. However, the June year-to-date total repre-
> sents an expense of $42.67 per employee.

Most reviewers would accept this as a reasonable explanation, but it really isn't. The critical question that should be

asked at this point is: Now that you've discovered your department is running over budget, what are you going to do about it?

Since you can't depend on someone else to ask the right question, you must take action on your own. The right action will depend on the account. We have used office supplies for our example, because it's one account most likely to present variance problems for you.

Each expense must be analyzed by its nature. For example, variable expenses should be compared to the volume of sales, since they must be expected to change on that criterion. However, variables often are budgeted in isolation from income forecasts. Thus, no effective controls will be possible.

Example: The marketing manager of one company compared travel expenses to gross sales each month and developed a percentage ratio to spot the expense trends. The original budget assumed that travel expenses would average 5 percent of each month's sales volume. An analysis for six months is shown in Figure 13-3.

The average travel expense per month is rising as a percentage of sales. If the budget assumption is realistic, this account is showing a negative trend. When comparing expenses to sales, you must be aware of distortions that can be caused by timing. For example, one month's sales might represent payments for activity occurring in a previous month, or income might be accrued in advance of related travel expenses. In addition, the travel expense itself might not be reported in the books for the same period the sales show up.

To correct these problems with complete accuracy, it would be desirable to relate the expense to the related income as a basis for comparison. But even with a highly sophisticated computer system in place, this idea would require extra encoding of both elements and might not produce enough additional information to be of any real value.

You will be able to allow for monthly distortions by reporting variable expenses on average. Both the year-to-date

Figure 13-3.
Variable expense analysis.

MONTH	TRAVEL EXPENSES	GROSS SALES	RATIO
Jan	$3,415	$74,530	4.6%
Feb	4,155	73,910	5.6
Mar	3,982	78,054	5.1
Apr	4,510	75,183	6.0
May	3,901	72,288	5.4
Jun	4,732	80,216	5.9

expense and year-to-date gross sales are summarized on an average basis, with the following formula:

Step 1:
$$\frac{\text{Year-to-date expense}}{\text{Number of months}} = \text{Average monthly expense}$$

Step 2:
$$\frac{\text{Year-to-date sales}}{\text{Number of months}} = \text{Average monthly sales}$$

Step 3:
$$\frac{\text{Average monthly expense}}{\text{Average monthly sales}} = \text{Ratio}$$

When each month's ratio is compared with the average, a more dependable trend will emerge. As the year progresses, a single month's distortion will be minimized by the size of the field in the average.

ESTABLISHING BASIC EXPENSE CONTROLS

Controls are best derived from current information. As long as you can identify the problem, the solution will become more obvious. Thus, to establish an expense control, you must first develop an analysis of each month's activity. Guidelines for this analysis are:

- It must be simple enough to produce without spending a great deal of time. An overly complicated analysis takes time away from other tasks and will offset any savings you will create.
- The comparison should be made between actual expenses and the budget. Current month expenses should be broken down into subclassifications coordinated with original assumptions.
- The analysis must include details in the current month and should be followed with an explanation of causes.

Because each expense account will contain different transaction levels and varying degrees of budgeting difficulty, the analysis itself must be flexibly designed. The form you complete should be modified to suit the nature of the account. Figure 13-4 shows a sample account analysis form. This form allows room for actual, budget, and variance summaries. In order to break the account down in this way, you must be able to identify current payments by assumption groups. At the bottom of the form, each component of the variance should be summarized.

With a similar form used for each account, you will be able to explain departmental variances with little difficulty. However, the form does not have to be completed each month or for every expense your department incurs. Concentrate on problem accounts or accounts with especially large budgets. The remainder are likely to have only minor variances, and the time required to analyze them will not be justified.

For relatively low-budget and low-transaction accounts, the analysis can be less formal. You should review all transactions assigned to your department or generated by your subordinates. Look for unusual expenses, for coding errors, or for allocated expenses you did not expect. Then

Figure 13-4.
Account analysis form.

Account Variance Worksheet

Month _____

Account _____

Department _____

	ACTUAL	BUDGET	VARIANCE
Previous year-to-date			
Assumption categories:			
_____			
_____			
_____			
_____			
_____			
_____			
total, current month			
total, year-to-date			

Components of variance:

_____

_____

_____

_____

_____

_____

_____

complete your investigation by reviewing any transactions that don't look right to you.

Account analysis does not have to take up a lot of time in your department. You can take several steps to reduce the time this procedure demands:

- Analyze only those accounts in which you have experienced significant variances in the past.
- Review coding of transactions on a weekly or daily basis by careful study of check requests that pass through your office and by an examination of disbursement reports throughout the month.
- Institute approval and coding procedures to prevent discovered errors from repeating. Don't simply make a correction. Identify the source of recurring errors and make changes to prevent them in the future.

THE BUDGET AS A MARKETING TOOL

The budgeting process (including income forecasts, expense budgets, and cash flow projections) can be used as a marketing tool in several ways. By "marketing," we mean not only serving an outside customer or client. Remember that several departments serve an internal market. One example is the accounting department, whose "customer" is top management and every other manager in the company.

Budgets can support a proposal for revised procedures, for new products or services, or expansion of markets. As a manager, you have opportunities to present ideas to decision makers. And using budgetary information helps you to market your ideas.

In a marketing department, where at least the preliminary work for income forecasts is prepared, the process can be used for a direct version of marketing. Using proper assumptions, a forecast should be based on factors that can be tracked and controlled. For example, in an environment in which individual salespeople or sales offices move product to the market, the forecast should be based on assumptions related to average production per individual, recruitment plans, and regional factors.

When the forecast is properly developed, the marketing department gains two advantages. First, the forecast can be monitored. That means that if actual income falls below the forecast, the causes can be identified and action can then be taken. Second, the forecast could be built from exact details per salesperson—in effect, a series of individual goals for the coming year. Then, the forecast not only serves for monthly review, but also as the basis for field motivation and leadership.

Example: The marketing manager is preparing a forecast for next year. Through a series of discussions with field managers, he develops a tentative quota for each salesperson. These are reviewed in the field and some modifications are made. In the end, each field representative knows what the company expects for the coming year, in terms of numbers of customer contacts, orders placed, and sales volume.

Next, the marketing manager studies recruitment trends and attrition rates. Using averages for first-year salespeople, he estimates reasonable goals for new people, which will be used in the interview phase as well as for month-to-month variance study. The manager estimates the number of existing salespeople who are likely to leave during the year and reduces the forecast by the average production per person for the past year.

An income forecast variance report (see Figure 13-5 for a sample worksheet) should break down each month's actual and budget totals by the assumption base. So if the forecast was built from individual quotas or goals, a variance report must compare the estimates to actual performance. Follow-up action should include checking progress with individuals falling below their personal goals. A field manager will be responsible for motivating these individuals to meet agreed-upon sales levels and to catch up with year-to-date production quotas.

Figure 13-5.
Forecast variance reporting worksheet.

	ACTUAL	FORECAST	VARIANCE
Previous year–to–date			
Assumption categories:			

Income Forecast Variances

Month _____

Previous year–to–date

Assumption categories:

total, current month

total, year–to–date

Components of variance:

PLANNING AND CREATING PROFITS

Managers can create profits when budgets work. That's a substantial qualification, however, because in spite of the best intentions of individual managers, budgeting often fails in its primary purpose.

One way you can ensure that today's budget helps you to better participate in achieving your company's objective

Figure 13-6.
Budget memo.

Budget Memo

Date _____

Account _____
Department _____

Notes for future budgets:

Assumption base _____
_____
_____

Variances _____
_____
_____

Recommendations _____
_____
_____
_____
_____

---

is to set a standard for yourself: Everything you discover this year will be documented and carried over to next year, so that future budgets will be more complete. That means fine-tuning assumptions, picking up missing elements of an expense account, looking for future need to control expenses as an employee base expands, and noting the types of unexpected variances that arise.

Prepare a budget memo for your files whenever you find any problems with the current budget. For example, a transaction occurs that was completely overlooked, indicating that the assumptions were incomplete. Or one cause of unfavorable variances (such as timing of transactions versus budget months) occurs chronically. A budget memo should be placed in your file for next year's budget. A sample of this form is shown in Figure 13-6.

Budgeting is your scorekeeping standard. The process lets you determine whether your ability to predict the future is well developed and where you need more work. It defines your financial goals and then provides the means for tracking them. But the budgeting process is more than just a task. It is the operational vehicle for realizing the goals in your company's business plan.

The plan begins with the premise that a target can be reached in the future. This target might be a marketing expansion, a level of gross sales or net profits, a new product or service, or improvement in capital position. These "big picture" goals are put on a timetable and tested for feasibility. Then, the final plan is expressed in terms of operating budgets. When top management guides its departments within the context of the plan, budgets become more than an administrative routine; they become the action that achieves the planned goals of the company.

Chapter 14

The Departmental System

A successful business operates according to a plan. But the plan does not exist only on the companywide level or in the executive wing. Each manager contributes to the overall success of the plan. Every department must understand its role in achieving the goals expressed for the entire company. If this year's sales are planned to be higher, the marketing department tracks volume and sales activity in the field; the administrative departments ensures that orders are processed and filled, records updated, and reports prepared; and support departments gear up for higher volume. Every department plays a part in the planning.

Managers need to devise a departmental plan that addresses its role in the company goals. And in many circumstances, a plan is designed to achieve a goal outside of the larger plan, to solve problems that affect only one department or to improve procedures now in place. In any of these cases, control procedures should achieve several purposes:

1. Reach the department's goals according to the company's business plan or based on a specific assignment given to the manager.
2. Identify department and employee goals and then track progress so that they will be met.
3. Monitor cooperation with other departments to make sure that plan-oriented work stays on schedule.

THE NEED FOR CONTROLS

A basic question to answer regarding "controls" is, Exactly what are they? The word is used extensively in business, but could have several definitions. It's often the case that no one is really sure what a control is, or what purpose it serves. A control procedure should be designed to ensure that an end result is achieved. This assumes that without the control, that end result is not possible or that some other outcome will occur.

Example: You attend a budget review meeting, where it's revealed that your department's office supply expense is running 20 percent above budget. You are instructed to initiate a control procedure to reduce spending. That may consist of a preapproval, a requisition system, a reduction in per-employee use, or even locking up the supplies used in your department.

Example: The sales manager is told that this year's forecast calls for a 5 percent increase in volume. He decides to track sales volume with a monthly quota for each salesperson, with the annual total coordinated to the 5 percent increase.

Example: The customer service department manager wants to improve response time to customer inquiries, complaints, and service requests. She devises a review and tracking system, starting with the letter or phone call received, then the follow-up action, and finally, the end result. This system will help the manager identify the cause of delays in response time.

In each of these examples, the manager devised a method for achieving a specific goal. A control cannot be effective unless a desired result is first known. The control procedure must have several attributes:

1. The purpose must be clear. The manager cannot know what to control or how to control it until a problem is identified and a goal established. For example, an expense must be reduced to conform to the budget, sales activity must be monitored to achieve a forecast total, or customer contact and response time must be tracked to identify causes of delay.

2. The control must be monitored. A control serves no purpose unless it is monitored. Thus, for a control to work, it must first be possible to track results and to know what those results mean. This element is often missing in the creation of controls but is an essential point that cannot be forgotten. Second, the monitoring process must be executed. It does no good to identify a problem and create a control, unless you do follow-up and make sure the process is installed.

3. The control must be practical. The controls you devise and install must be realistic, in terms of time demands and results. A control should be simple and efficient. If the process of controlling places too great a demand on your time or on the time and tasks of someone else, it probably cannot succeed.

4. Discovered flaws must be corrected. Controls often are designed to uncover problems. For example, a budget control might find the source of overspending. Or a customer service tracking procedure might find a weak link in the follow-up and response to requests. When those problems are found, the responsible manager must take action to eliminate the causes or to change the element that creates them.

THE ACCOUNTING APPROACH

Every manager faces the problem of putting effective controls in place. After discovering the *need* for controls, and even after identifying the steps that must be taken, how do you successfully get others to act? And how do you ensure that the monitoring steps are followed?

Every manager can learn from the approach taken by the accountant. Part of the accountant's task is to record and report, but another part is a tracking function. Accountants are trained to identify and watch trends and to develop solutions to negative trends as they emerge. You can apply the same discipline in a nonfinancial environment. Accountants work with numbers, so their trend-watching involves black-and-white data. Compared to some of the less tangible problems you must confront, number-related problems might seem fairly simple. The truth is, this accounting function is quite complex and requires experience and deft action.

Example: The manager of the accounting department tracks overhead expenses for the first quarter and identifies several potential problems. He then contacts managers in several departments to discuss control possibilities.

In this example, the accountant has attempted to identify areas of emerging problems. The difficulty will be in communicating a concern to a nonaccounting manager and in gaining cooperation and agreement on the course of action that should be taken today. For the accountant, this task is challenging and formidable.

First is the problem of working with someone who is probably not oriented to finance. So the accountant must serve in the role of educator and also must contend with the attitude that accountants are preoccupied with financial analysis. Second is the chance that another manager will feel defensive in being asked to develop controls, or even to participate in control monitoring: Accountants meet a great deal of resistance in their effort to gain cooperation from other managers. Third is the problem of follow-through: The accountant depends on cooperation in order for controls to work.

You can learn from the accounting approach to the control process and apply those skills within your own department. Your advantage in many cases is that you do not have to confront other departments or educate others in the control process. If you're working with subordinates, you only need to make sure that they know their role in your departmental control system and what the system must achieve.

PUTTING CONTROLS INTO EFFECT

You can initiate your own controls, or they might be imposed on you from someone else. For example, you are aware of a problem in meeting deadlines and devise a method for speeding up work processes. Or, the executive in charge of your division asks you to speed up your transaction processing. In either case, the response actions will occur strictly within your department. Let's follow the process of identifying and completing a control action within a single department, using the same four steps that accountants employ in developing and completing their control actions when dealing with numbers: defining the purpose, monitoring, making it practical, and acting on discovered flaws.

Example: The vice-president instructs you to cut down on the level of office supply expenses in your department. After four months in the current year, your department reports an unfavorable variance of 15 percent above the budget.

Step 1. Purpose

Begin the process by ensuring that the purpose of the control action is well understood. Without this important step, you might put a great deal of energy and time into your process, only to later discover that you did not achieve the intended goal.

When a control requirement is imposed on you, it will be necessary to discuss the intended purpose. What does someone else want to achieve? Without knowing this, you cannot take the next step—determining how to enact the appropriate control.

For the assignment to reduce office supply expenses, you need to know the following: Is the purpose of the control to ensure that the variance does not continue? Or does the vice-president want you to eliminate the variance completely, so that by the end of the year, you're within the budget? And what deadline should be assigned for (1) identifying the control measures you must take, and (2) completion of the goal?

After you know what must be achieved, the control action will usually be obvious. Assuming that the vice-president only wants the variances to stop, your task must be to ensure the monthly budget level is not exceeded. You discover that the problem comes from several circumstances. First, at the beginning of the year, you purchased a one-year supply of one expensive item. Second, employees in your department have been allowed to order supplies whenever they wanted, without coordination and without prior approval.

These circumstances point the way to a solution. The one-year supply purchase will be absorbed over the coming year, so part of the variance should disappear over time. Thus, your actual expenses can be reduced, on average, by absorption. Second, your control of ongoing expenses should consist of preapproval at the very least. You decide to put one employee in charge of coordination within the department. All employees are told to convey their supply needs to the responsible person, who will place an order once a week. You will then review and approve the order before it is placed.

Step 2. Monitoring

Once a control procedure has been identified and the right actions taken to put it in place, you must next be able to track progress. What will you discover and what reaction is required?

In the first week, you discover part of the problem. Several employees have ordered identical supplies, and by combining the order, a better price can be obtained from the supplier. It occurs to you that by combining the ordering process with other departments, even greater savings can be achieved. In addition, you question whether the supplies on the list should be purchased from the supplier the company uses each month. Is it possible that a better price is available from another?

You contact three other managers and suggest that supply could be centralized and thus better controlled. The managers are receptive to the idea, especially if that would mean removing individual responsibility from their departments.

You also speak with the employee in charge of purchasing and ask for a price comparison from other suppliers.

Step 3. Practical controls

The employee in charge of control complains that it is taking a lot of time. Thus, she is not able to complete her other tasks. In response, you reassign some of those tasks, at least temporarily, to relieve pressure on the employee. The assignment to compare prices puts an even greater time demand on the employee. You respond by stating that this is a one-time task, made necessary only by what you have discovered by checking the weekly order.

Step 4. Acting on discovered flaws

You now know that other managers like the idea of combining the supply purchasing. You also know how much time is required to perform that duty just for your department. Assuming that the same time commitment exists in other departments as well, you conclude that a centralized supply department makes sense.

When your employee completes her price comparison, you discover that savings can be achieved with a little shopping around. However, it isn't always practical to call four or five supplies for every item on the list. Here again, a centralized procedure will make the entire process more efficient.

Your actions include the following:

1. You instruct your employee to place orders where the lowest prices are offered.

2. You prepare a report summarizing the time demands of supply purchasing and control and discussing the savings made possible by price comparison. Comparing your department's supply budget to the budget for the whole company, you estimate the overall savings that would be possible by centralizing the process. The report makes a case for creation of a new supply department.
3. You meet again with several other managers and show them your first draft. They add their ideas and you prepare a revised version.
4. You submit your report to the vice-president who gave you the original assignment.
5. You summarize your discoveries and the actions you have taken to date. You also give this summary to the vice-president. In the report, you state that you have put controls in place that will keep your spending within the budget and that the 15 percent variance will be at least partially offset by savings throughout the year and by absorbing the previous one-year supply purchase.

In this example, an isolated problem in one department led to the discovery of a solution that could affect many more people and departments. Assuming that every other manager faces similar control problems, centralizing the monitoring and budget controls might enable the company to save money, not only in the level of supply costs, but also by reducing each department's time demands.

COMMUNICATING WITH OTHER DEPARTMENTS

The process of initiating and following up on controls is more complex when other departments are involved. You must not only identify the means for a solution; you will also depend on cooperation and follow-up from others. It's extremely difficult and politically volatile to impose your control ideas on others. But if you approach the problem from the other manager's viewpoint, cooperation is more likely. As long as your control ideas solve a problem for another department, it's in the manager's own interests to work with you.

Example: You submit a report to management recommending the creation of a centralized supply department. The response is favorable. However, before the new department is created, the vice-president instructs you to study budget and expense trends in your department and three others. The conclusion should demonstrate how much can be saved.

This change requires analyzing expense levels and budget variances in other departments and then estimating the savings from creating a new department. These savings must be compared to the expense—paying a salary to at least one person and committing floor space to a centralized supply area. In addition, procedures will have to be developed, requisition forms designed, and initial contacts with vendors established. All of this represents an investment on the part of the company. The questions are: Will that investment be justified, and how long will it take to recapture the initial expense?

Your task is a form of control, as well as the research for an assigned report. However, in this case, you will depend on help from other managers. Remembering that the issues must be presented so that they will benefit, you will need to emphasize the positive points when asking for cooperation.

One approach is to simply ask for help. However, this approach is not likely to create an enthusiastic response. You could also ask permission to study past expenses and budgets in other departments and do all of the work yourself. But that would exclude the observations, insights, and ideas that other managers can offer, making your report less comprehensive than you'd like.

The best approach is to meet with each manager, explain the benefits of centralizing the process, and then ask for their help. The information you need is not complex and will not be time-consuming to put together. If another manager is willing to spend time in analysis, you should welcome that help. However, since it's your assignment, you must also be prepared to accept raw information and work from there.

If you do not receive the timely cooperation you'd like, you might have to proceed without it. While this means your report will be less comprehensive than you'd like, that's better than being late with the assignment. Be prepared to work around others if necessary, to do much of the work yourself, or to repeat your request when someone else is holding up your schedule.

DEALING WITH PROBLEMS

You will face three problems in putting a new control system in place. They are the same problems you will face for preparing reports, taking part in meetings, managing a long-term project, or performing any other task that requires interaction within the company. These problems are:

1. Missed deadlines. When you create a control, it must be defined in the context of a specific goal that must have a deadline. The deadline might be imposed on you—for example, an executive wants results or a report on your control system within one month. It might also be a secondary deadline within a larger project—for example, you are performing a control study for centralizing the supply function and you need information from other managers.

Don't wait until the last minute to discover whether a deadline will be missed. When you give a deadline to someone else, leave yourself a few days to react in case the information is late. Also keep in touch between the assignment and deadline dates to avoid surprises.

2. Flawed assumptions. Controls will succeed only when the original assumptions are correct. For example, if you are given the assignment to reduce expenses in your department, you might assume that an unfavorable variance must be eliminated, that drastic control measures are mandated, or that your department is the only one creating the problem.

In reality, all of these assumptions could be flawed. The existing variance might be within an acceptable range and is not expected to go away. The solution might not require a complicated control procedure but could be resolved quickly and simply. And other departments might contribute to the problem, so that the needed control is not entirely within your power to create.

Another flawed assumption might be found in the budget itself. For example, the level of spending in your department might be reasonable but the budget is unrealistic. If you study the issues and find that the real problem is other than what it appears to be, your response should be to point out the flawed assumption—along with the right proof, of course.

3. Lack of cooperation. When you need help from someone else but they resist giving it or, even worse, passively fail to respond, you face a difficult task. Not only must you respond with appropriate control actions, you must also resolve the problem of the uncooperative manager.

Accountants face this problem frequently. In every function they perform, they depend on financial information from other departments, and that information is not always turned in willingly or on time. They often must work around others, get help through the chain of command, or appeal to outside managers two or three times.

When your control procedure involves other departments, build a foundation of cooperation by meeting with the managers involved and explaining what you're trying to accomplish. Point out the advantages to them and ask for a commitment. Give deadlines for response, using all the diplomacy you can muster, recognizing that few of us like getting assignments from other managers. If necessary, go through the chain of command to force cooperation, but use this as a last resort, and only if your other diplomatic efforts fail.

CHANGING CONTROLS

The day will come when a control procedure must be updated and revised, or even eliminated. As part of the monitoring process you initiate, look for signs that changes are necessary and keep the process flexible enough to modify with circumstances.

An initial control procedure will probably involve much research. Alternative solutions must be studied, historical facts must be gathered and analyzed, trends must be studied so that the right conclusion is drawn. After that, the process is relatively simple. But over time, the information itself might become outdated.

The control function is a familiar task to accountants. On the basis of numbers—analysis, trend-watching, and reporting—controls are a constant routine. The whole financial reporting process is a control, as it tells management whether they are earning a profit and return on investment and whether the goals expressed in the forecast and budget are being met.

You can use the same techniques of defining and solving problems to create controls in your department and, at the same time, ensure that the process does not become a bureaucratic, paper-heavy routine. By keeping the control system as simple as possible, and by following up with the right actions, control within your department will be a manageable, effective process.

Afterword

In this book, no distinction has been made between the many roles played by the accountant. These distinctions are not important, since the concern here is only with the application of accounting skills in a nonaccounting environment. But like the accountant, you, too, must perform in several roles as a manager.

First, you need to act as an effective supervisor and leader, with sensitivity, insight, and self-confidence.

Second, you need to communicate with other employees through discussions with one other person, meetings of various sizes, and the messages you convey in memos, letters, and reports.

Third, you are a member of the organization "family," a part of the corporate culture. You want to survive the political power moves—the corporate version of sibling rivalry. This atmosphere is natural and the political climate in your company helps define who the players are, and the role they play.

Fourth, you share a scorekeeping duty with everyone else in the company. Some people readily admit that the company exists to make a profit and outperform the competition. Yet, when it comes to their role, they resist the idea of improving the environment in which profits will occur. In some way, the idea of money is perceived as distasteful.

There is no conflict between the human or intangible side of your job and the black-and-white, less human concern with finance and profits. The conflict arises when two managers confront a single issue with different priorities. But with understanding and cooperation, that conflict can be resolved.

ROLES AND RESPONSIBILITY

You can reconcile your different roles by resolving to work with others in a constructive manner. This applies in every instance when two or more people get together. Working with your company's accountant is much easier once you understand his or her role, on two levels:

1. The accountant's product. First, the accountant's product is the numbers. This does not mean accountants have a limited perspective on human issues, only that their outlet is communication of historical fact and estimation of the future, all involving financial information. Within that role, the accounting manager also deals with a series of human issues, both within the accounting department and on the outside.

2. Management's expectations. Top management often labels accountants as exceptionally capable and dependable resources. Accuracy, perception, and the ability to predict future trends all are assumed, and top management comes to depend on accountants for these qualities. But when accountants perform several different roles or when they specialize narrowly, the expectation often proves misplaced.

For accountants, this level of assumption also creates pressure. It puts them in the middle. Top management expects results, even when its assumptions are not realistic. At the same time, other managers see the accountant as an enforcer or seeker of power. These problems make the accountant's job difficult.

Even when top management does not verbalize its dependence on the accountant, the fact often remains that the accountant is expected to accurately predict what will happen, based only on the numbers, and to see the "big picture" to a greater degree than other managers.

Don't make a distinction of responsibility. If you think that your role is strictly nonfinancial and that only the accountant deals with financial matters, you have already given up a part of the role you should be accepting. You will lose a degree of authority you should have, as well as a voice in the organization that *every* manager needs in order to participate.

Your responsibility belongs to all four roles you play: leader, communicator, member of the culture, and scorekeeper. If you give up on any of these, you also curtail your career opportunities. To progress in your company, you need to act as a versatile, well-rounded, and flexible manager who perceives problems with human, cultural, and financial solutions in mind, often expressed as "seeing things from someone else's point of view." In fact, it's actually an expansion of your own viewpoint.

SKILLS FOR ADVANCEMENT

The ability to perceive and communicate issues in financial terms certainly will help you in your career. We cannot ignore the impact of finance: To top management, it often tells the whole story. Your CEO, board of directors, and executives might be very concerned with quality of corporate life and morale. But they are under pressure to show progress over and above the previous year. So no matter what issue is on the table, top management must always ask, "What will it cost?"

Even the most human of issues can be addressed with financial concerns in mind. When you want approval for an idea, when you propose a change, and when you ask for a budget increase, the logic of your request might be obvious to you. By confronting the financial issues in your arguments, you will make a stronger argument, and you will help management to arrive at a sound decision.

You can achieve this balance as a manager/diplomat in an assertive manner and with confidence in the facts you present. You can prove your case with absolute clarity, and still present it in a brief moment of opportunity, among many other issues and pressures. If you want to make your point, you will have to identify the major decision points and present your case with diplomacy.

Once you're able to find that balance, you will be perceived as a capable professional, on a par with the best of accountants. You can combine the human and the financial viewpoint in making your case, so that your responsibilities to your department *and* to the bottom line can be satisfied in a single argument.

You can anticipate future needs, plan for them, and communicate with management in the context of the company's plan. Take responsibility, participate, and think of yourself as an expert whose job includes acting as an informed consultant to the organization. Then build your case for solutions with indisputable facts and with an eye on profitability.

PROBLEMS OF THE POWER BASE

Company life would be a fairly simple matter if power were not constantly at issue. For example, the accountants in your organization might be terribly unhappy with the role top management has imposed. They're in the middle. Yet, if you propose changing the power structure, you might also run into fierce resistance.

Any change will be perceived as a threat, and a great deal of energy will go into arguing against it, especially when the idea takes power away from someone else.

The instinctive desire to retain power and to increase it will always impede your efforts, no matter what your motivation. You might suggest a decentralized budgeting system, for example, which would simplify the accountant's life. But the reaction might be negative. It is naive to assume that everyone will appreciate your ideas and see them from your viewpoint.

You gain considerable ground in your effort when you first present your ideas to the accounting department. If you are able to first convince the accountant that the plan makes sense, you will have overcome the greatest difficulty you face. Whenever you are able to create an alliance between yourself and the accounting department, your task will be much easier.

Avoid surprising people in meetings or through your efforts at communication. If a suggestion involves changing the role of another department, first speak to the manager and explain your viewpoint. Emphasize the benefits to the other manager, and try to build an argument with common interests.

You will not be able to completely eliminate the problems involving the desire for a power base. If the accounting department now has a great deal of power and influence in the company, you can expect change to occur only over time, through gradual modification rather than sweeping revision. It certainly helps to have the accountant as an ally, but in many situations you cannot depend on that happening.

The best way to equalize power or to better distribute it in the company is to demonstrate to top management that you're a professional, capable manager who is constantly aware of the numbers. This attribute does not have to remain exclusive with Accounting. It can be shared by everyone, from Accounting to the nonfinancial departments in the company.

CONFIDENCE THROUGH MASTERY

In any field, confidence comes from gaining knowledge and skill. There's nothing like success to build self-esteem and to motivate us to continue along the right path. At the same time, a good deal of what we learn comes from making mistakes and from improving future performance by developing away from past attempts.

In developing financial insights and using the techniques practiced by accountants in a nonaccounting environment, you will also learn through doing. The specific techniques are not difficult to master; they're only the principles of good business habits. You have the advantage in the fact that your product or service is not strictly involved with the black and white of financial information.

Practice the skills and techniques that accountants use, paying close attention to these five ideas:

1. Document your facts and prove your case. Always assume that your premise will be questioned, even when doubts are not verbalized. Your viewpoint will not be accepted automatically, and even the most logical, obvious case must be proved beyond a doubt. You will need to develop skill in selecting and interpreting facts, an ability that will improve with practice.

2. Always consider the financial question. No matter what point you're trying to make, there will always be a financial side to the issue. If you don't address that side of the issue, your proposal might be rejected. Always address the question of profits, return on investment, and financial necessity when you present ideas.

3. Think of the accountant as an ally. Avoid the adversarial mentality that often grows in companies between accountants and other departments. Once you begin communicating with the accountant, both viewpoints will be enriched and expanded. That frees the communication channel and makes it easier for both sides to come to the best possible conclusion.

4. Practice and apply ideas. You cannot expect to adopt a different point of view overnight or to apply accounting skills in your department without hard work. These capabilities and their application will be developed over time and will be fine-tuned only through practice. Any skill worth developing will be gained with determination.

5. Become a manager/diplomat. Always be aware of sensitivity, notably in Accounting. That's a high-pressure job, with deadlines and demands from all sides constantly at issue. When a suggestion appears to invade the accountants' circle of influence or to threaten their power base, they will react in a human way. Be sure that your message is delivered clearly and with sensitivity. Try speaking with the accountant before you present an idea in a meeting. Explain your point of view. Ask for ideas and suggestions.

By accepting the idea that all of your tasks, priorities, and goals have a financial side, you will be well on the way to furthering your management skills. You will then discover that you and the accountant are on the same team, share common goals, and want the same end result.

Appendix A

The Double-Entry System

Mastering financial skills depends on a general comprehension of accounting disciplines. You do not need to perfect detailed skills involved with bookkeeping, but an overview of the double-entry system will aid communication between you and the accountant.

When a financial statement is presented for review, you see only the end result. But supporting the summarized numbers is a completely verified series of routines. By the time a statement is committed to paper, a number of preliminary stages have been completed. All of these are based on detailed records kept in Accounting.

BASICS OF THE SYSTEM

Modern accounting practice includes use of the double-entry system. On a management level, the accountant is probably not involved in the actual details but depends on the records and control procedures produced by bookkeepers and accounting clerks.

Double-entry means just that: Every transaction has two equal sides and is posted twice. The left side is the debit and the right side is the credit. The credit will appear in red or in brackets, but that does not indicate a negative value. The only purpose of debits and credits is to distinguish one side from the other.

Example: The income account normally contains a credit balance. It is not negative income, but reflects an accumulating balance of credit-side entries. The same is true of liability accounts. When money is owed, a liability contains a credit balance.

Posting every entry twice might seem like unnecessary duplication of effort, until you study the nature of any transaction. When you receive income, you increase the balance of the income account; you must also show a corresponding increase in cash (or, if sold on account, an increase to the accounts receivable asset). When you pay an expense, you increase the expense account balance, and offset that entry with a reduction (credit) to your cash account. Without exception, every transaction affects two different accounts.

The double-entry system is designed to ensure a control feature lacking in other systems. Because debits and credits must always be equal, the books must always add up to zero. When debits are added and credits subtracted, a correctly posted set of books will balance out. If any math errors have occurred, they'll show up when balances are tested.

Example: A bookkeeper makes a math error, either in recording one side of a transaction, or in adding the balance of an account. When all balances are checked, the sum of accounts' values do not equal zero.

Just as the totals of all entries must be zero, the balances of all accounts will also show equal entries to each side. If the total of a ledger's debit-balance accounts does not equal the total of all credit-balance accounts, there's an error somewhere in the books.

This control feature does not prevent entries from being posted to the wrong account. However, review procedures in Accounting should be designed to audit coding and posting periodically. That's an issue of quality control.

TYPES OF RECORDS

The detail and organization of each stage in the bookkeeping process becomes increasingly summarized. Source documents may number in the hundreds or thousands, including invoices, receipts, vouchers, and other papers. At that level, it would be impossible to analyze and draw conclusions about the financial condition of the company; yet, every entry should be supported with a source document as proof that it's a legitimate business transaction.

The second level is the books of original entry, consisting of several journals. These classify and summarize the source documents. Each transaction is recorded in a journal, and a summarized total is later posted to the general ledger. There are three types of journals:

1. Receipts journal, also called the cash or income journal, used for recording cash sales and sales on account, as well as cash receipts.
2. Disbursements journal, a summary of all money paid out from the company's checking accounts. The entries are normally recorded in check-number sequence, and monthly totals added up and posted.
3. General journal, used to enter transactions that do not fit into the format of either of the other two journals. For example, entries will be made here to record depreciation (a noncash expense); to accrue accounts payable (a liability not yet paid but due); or to correct a discovered error.

The last level in the books is the general ledger, also called the books of final entry. This is the most summarized of all stages. At the most, each account should contain no more than a balance forward, summarized entries from one or more of the three journals, and an ending balance. The general ledger should hold as little detail as possible to make it more practical to maintain balance control and to draw financial statements.

The flow of records is summarized in Figure A-1.

ACCOUNTING METHODS

Entries can be recorded in one of two accounting methods. Under the *cash accounting* method, an entry is made only

Figure A-1.
Records summary.

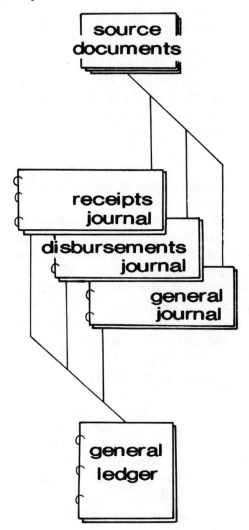

when cash changes hands. Under the *accrual accounting* method, income is recorded when it's earned, and costs and expenses are recorded when incurred, regardless of when cash actually is exchanged.

The advantage in cash accounting is its simplicity. There is no need to report money that's due or owed. The big disadvantage is that cash accounting is inaccurate. If a payment or receipt is delayed by a few days, a financial statement will not show the true condition of the company.

Example: On a cash basis, the books show a profit for the month of $8,415. But the accounting department is holding unpaid invoices totaling more than $10,000. If these were included in the current financial statement, it would show a net loss rather than a profit.

Accrual accounting is more complex because income must be recorded if earned (even if it hasn't yet been paid), and all incurred costs and expenses must also be shown. That means having to keep track not only of what has occurred to date, but what's expected in the future. Accrual accounting is essential in most operations, because current financial information must be realistic. In a large organization, with thousands, even millions of dollars in receivables and payables, the impact of pending transactions cannot be ignored.

The following is an example of how cash and accrual accounting compare:

1. Income of $4,000 is earned in the month of May but is not paid until June.
2. Telephone expense of $285 is incurred during the month of June, but the bill is not paid until July.

Figure A-2 shows how these entries would be treated under each accounting method. Depending on the size of the accruals involved, a delay in recording under the cash method can make a tremendous difference in financial reports.

Accrual accounting provides a consistency that is both

Figure A-2.
Cash and accrual accounting.

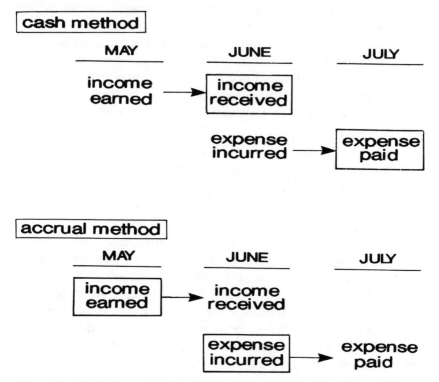

desirable and necessary. It provides the basis for dependable reporting in the following ways:

1. Determining what is in an account from one period to another is meaningful only when books are maintained in a consistent manner, with entries recorded in the proper and applicable period, not just as they are paid.
2. Trends, both favorable and unfavorable, can be better recognized and tracked when information is consistently recorded and reported.
3. Profits reported under the accrual basis tend to reflect the true state of affairs, while cash accounting can vary for a number of reasons.

RECORDING ENTRIES

Each time an accrual entry is made, it must later be followed by a reversal. For example, a liability is accrued this month and paid next month. When the bill is paid, the liability is eliminated, so the accrual is no longer valid. The accrual can be removed either by coding a payment against the accrual account or by preparing a reversing journal entry.

Example: A liability is set up at the end of the month, consisting of four bills the company owes. As they are paid, each one is coded as a debit to the liability account and a credit to the cash account. When all four payments have been made, the liability account balance should be zero.

Ensuring that accruals are reversed in this manner can be more work than it's worth. The bookkeeper must remember to code payments correctly, not as an expense but as a debit to a liability account. It's much easier to assign the payment to the proper expense account and prepare a reversing journal entry.

Example: A liability is set up by way of an accrual journal, consisting of four bills the company owes. In the following month, these four bills, along with many other current expenses, are paid and coded to the appropriate expense account category. A reversing journal is prepared to remove the previous month's reported liability.

Referring back to the accrual and cash comparison, how would accruals be entered for the $4,000 income and $285 telephone expense? Each would be accrued during the month earned or incurred and reversed as cash is exchanged. Figure A-3 shows how a series of journal entries would accomplish the accrual and reversal of these transactions.

Accruals are designed to place all changes in the proper month. You can review the effects of accruing entries by studying a summarized version of them. Figure A-4 shows how the two transactions and subsequent reversals de-

Figure A-3.
Accrual entries.

DATE	ACCOUNT	✓	DEBIT	CREDIT
	-1-			
5–31	accounts receivable		4,000.00	
	income			4,000.00
	-2-			
6–30	telephone expense		285.00	
	accounts payable			285.00
	-3-			
6–30	cash		4,000.00	
	accounts receivable			4,000.00
	-4-			
7–31	accounts payable		285.00	
	cash			285.00

scribed above will affect cash, accounts receivable, accounts payable, income, and expenses.

Figure A-4 shows an informal summary of the general ledger called the *T-account*. While actual books are not kept in this manner, the T-account enables you to review the effects of a series of transactions. In this instance:

1. The cash account shows money received and paid during the applicable months.
2. The accounts receivable account shows the amount outstanding at the end of May, with payment occurring in June.
3. The accounts payable liability is outstanding at the end of June and is reversed in July.
4. Both income and telephone expense accounts show current increases during the months earned and incurred.

Figure A-4.
T accounts.

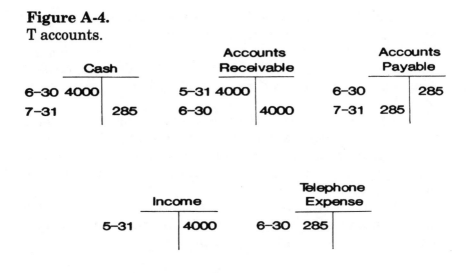

POSTING THE LEDGER

Once all entries to the three journals are added and balances verified, the totals are posted to the general ledger. On receipts and disbursements journals, a number of related transactions are summarized into single, month-end totals and posted that way.

Posting involves copying the total from each journal to the appropriate general ledger account. Many errors can occur during posting, and a bookkeeper's accuracy improves with experience. Examples of errors include:

1. Posting to the wrong account
2. Posting the wrong amount
3. Posting a debit as a credit, or vice versa
4. Adding or subtracting incorrectly
5. Failing to post an entry
6. Posting an entry twice
7. Failing to discover math errors in the journals, meaning debits and credits are not equal
8. Failing to verify correct balances forward, so that even a correctly posted and added ledger will never balance

Figure A-5 shows how a journal is recorded. On the journal, the column directly to the left of the debit column is checked when that entry has been made. This enables the bookkeeper to keep track of what has already been posted. And in the ledger, the "ref" column tells where the entry originated.

Accuracy of posting is verified by adding all the debit balances in the general ledger and subtracting all the credit balances. If the posting was done correctly, the total will come out as zero. But as long as it does not, the posting task is incomplete.

Most large companies now use automated processes for keeping books, so the job of manual recording is eliminated. Each transaction is entered in a program, which checks for

Figure A-5.
Posting to the ledger.

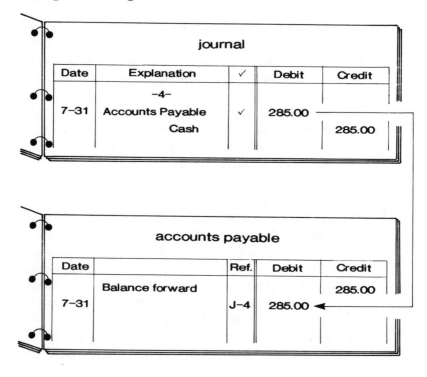

balance accuracy and automatically posts the general ledger. But automation does not solve the bookkeeper's problems, nor does it do away with the need for knowledge or accuracy. It only manages a volume of transactions more efficiently than human effort.

If an entry is entered incorrectly in an automated system, there is still a problem. The operator must understand how to correct the problem and how to minimize the frequency of errors.

THE SUBSIDIARY ACCOUNT

The three journals—receipts, disbursements, and general—each serve a specific purpose and are designed to handle certain types of transactions. In some cases, the volume is so great that an additional level is required.

Example: Your company sells most of its product on account. A large number of customers charge their purchases and are billed at the end of the month. During the following month, payments arrive and are recorded.

Keeping track of this activity on the usual receipts journal is not practical. You would not be able to track each customer's account activity. What's required, in addition to posting income and payments, is a system to capture each customer's account so that monthly bills can be prepared.

The solution is to create a subsidiary account, where each customer's charge and payment can be isolated and controlled. This subsidiary account, with one card per customer, becomes the basis for tracking activity for each customer, as well as for recording the cash, accounts receivable, and income totals that will eventually go into the general ledger. A master control sheet shows each entry, with a duplicate entry appearing on the customer's card. Payments are treated in the same way.

The totals of all charges and payments are balanced at

Figure A-6.
Subsidiary account.

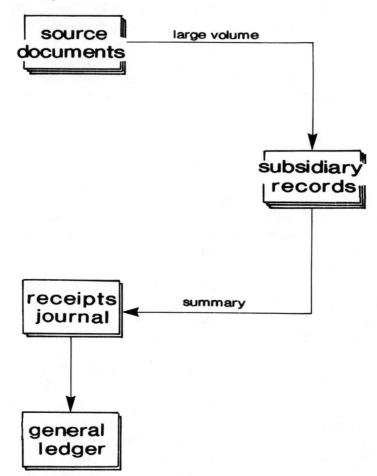

the end of the month to the details on customer cards, and summarized totals are then entered on the receipts journal. These totals are then posted to the general ledger. The flow of information with the use of a subsidiary account is shown in Figure A-6.

The premise of the bookkeeping and accounting system is that every transaction must be verified. It must be possible to trace all summarized values reported on the financial statement back through the system: to the general ledger, then to the appropriate journal entry, and finally to the source document.

Without that level of discipline, financial statements and the books that support them would always be questionable. However, with the concise rules for control and verification, accountants can present statements and other reports with a high degree of confidence.

Appendix B

The Financial Statement

Financial statements are reports summarizing a company's value as of a specific date, operating results for a period of time, or changes in cash balances. The statements are drawn from the records of transactions as summarized in the general ledger.

Accountants prepare reports beyond the three common financial statements. For example, a budget and forecast is an estimate of the future rather than a summary of the past. Other examples include:

1. A report that analyzes plant production with defect trends shown by shift
2. A one-time report summarizing the current value of real estate holdings
3. A report that breaks down the cost of hiring employees, including wages, benefits, and the cost to the company of maintaining the workplace

VALUE OF THE STATEMENT

Financial statements show past results and status. But they rarely tell the whole story, because they deal with a limited amount of information and must conform to rules for valuation. Excluded from the statement are current value of assets that might have been purchased several years ago but have since grown in value.

Example: Your company bought its headquarters building 10 years ago and paid $585,000. According to the books, its value today is only $350,000. Buildings are depreciated over a period of years, so that book value falls each year. However, real estate values have risen, and the current market value of the building is $700,000.

In this case, book value is only one-half of true value. Yet, the statement will not report the value in that way. The true financial picture of the company might be much different from what's reported in the financial statement.

The three types of financial statements are:

1. Balance sheet. A summary of the status and value of the company as of a specified date, the balance sheet lists assets, liabilities, and net worth. The sum of the assets is always equal to the sum of liabilities plus net worth.

2. Income statement. Also called the profit and loss statement, the income statement reports sales, direct costs, expenses, and profit over a period of time. The period ends with the same date that the balance sheet reports.

3. Statement of cash flows. This report shows the changes in cash balances over a period of time that conforms to the period covered by the income statement. Cash may be derived from revenues, the sale of assets, increases in long-term liabilities, or investment activities; it is spent on costs and expenses, inventory, increases in receivables and fixed assets, and income taxes.

Statements are drawn from the general ledger, which is set up in the same sequence that information is reported on the balance sheet and income statement. The ledger first lists assets, liabilities, and net worth (balance sheet accounts). After this come accounts for sales, direct costs, and general expenses (income statement accounts). The statement of cash flows compares beginning and ending balances in various accounts to show how cash was derived. Figure B-1 shows how general ledger accounts relate to the financial statements.

Figure B-1.
Financial statement sources.

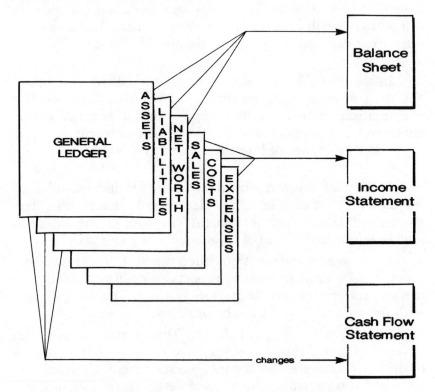

PREPARING FOR THE STATEMENTS

Financial statements are not merely copied from the general ledger account balances. First, a number of adjusting entries must be made, including:

1. Depreciation. Statements drawn during the year must include estimates of actual depreciation, which often is not computed precisely or booked until the end of the year.

2. Interest adjustments. As payments are made on notes, the month-to-month computation of interest might not be accurate. Before finalizing the statements, both the liability and interest expense account must be adjusted.

3. Bad debts. Some portion of accounts receivable might not be collectible, so a reserve for bad debts must be established and updated.

4. Changes in inventory. If the inventory level has changed since the last statement, an adjustment must be made, which also affects the cost of goods sold on the income statement.

This list by no means covers the entire range of possible adjustments that need to be made before statements can be drawn. Depending on circumstances, your accounting department might need to make a number of other accrual, reversal, or adjustment journal entries.

The first step in preparing financial statements is to draw a trial balance, which is a listing of all accounts in the general ledger. It proves that the books are in balance and also isolates the amount of profit being earned and reported to date. The net total of all asset, liability, and net worth accounts will add to the amount of profit. If the books are properly balanced, the net sum of sales, direct costs, and expense accounts will add to an identical balance. The trial balance format is shown in Figure B-2.

When statements are prepared before the end of the full year, the adjustments needed are made not in the general ledger but on a worksheet. Only month-to-month accruals and year-end final closing adjustments are actually entered into the general ledger. Figure B-3 shows an adjusting worksheet with the general ledger account balances shown in the first two columns. Following that are all adjusting journals, cross-referenced to supporting information, such as other worksheets used to compute the amount of the adjustment. The final two columns are the adjusted balances of each account, used to prepare the financial statements.

DRAWING THE STATEMENTS

Once the closing worksheet is complete, financial statements can be prepared. The balance sheet reports the current bal-

Figure B-2.
Trial balance.

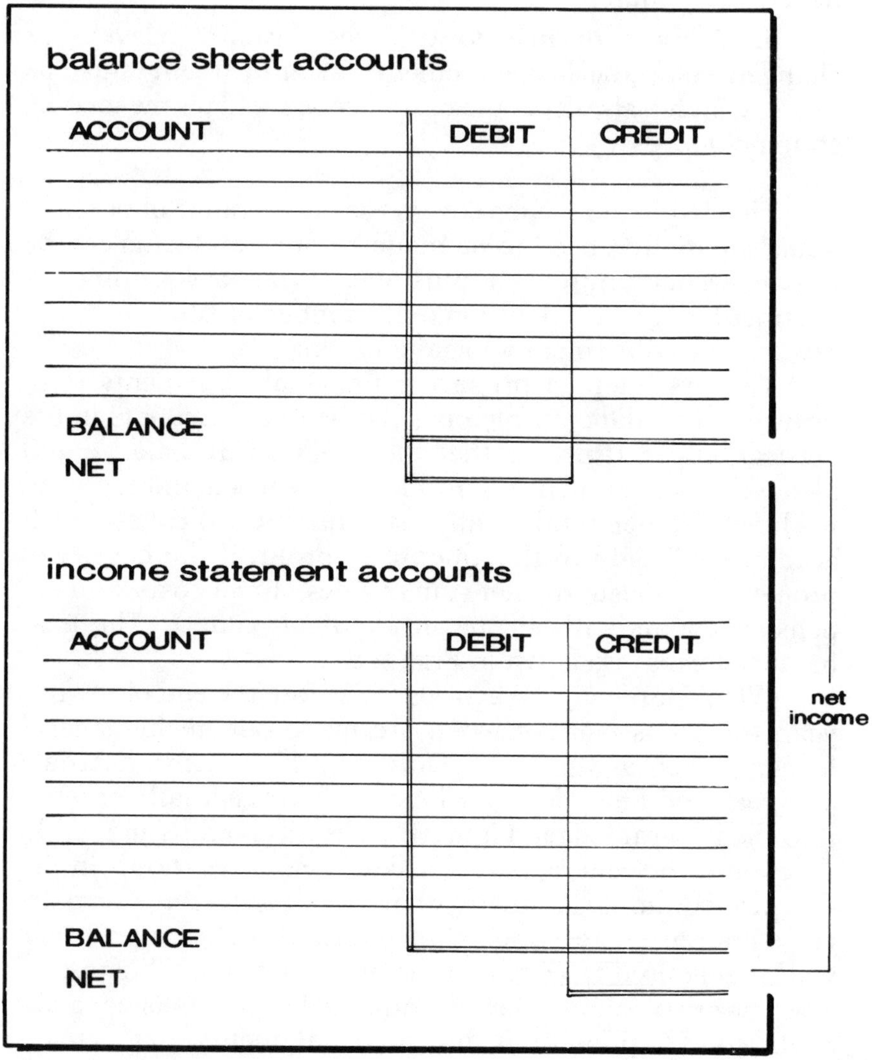

balance sheet accounts		
ACCOUNT	DEBIT	CREDIT
BALANCE		
NET		

income statement accounts		
ACCOUNT	DEBIT	CREDIT
BALANCE		
NET		

net
income

ances of each asset, liability, and net worth account, broken down into these subgroups:

Assets

- Current assets include cash and assets convertible to cash within one year.
- Long-term assets include furniture, equipment, land, buildings, and other capital assets, net of depreciation.
- Other assets include prepaid expenses, intangibles, and any assets that do not fit within the other groups.

Liabilities

- Current liabilities include all debts that are due and payable within twelve months.

Figure B-3.
Closing worksheet.

ACCOUNT	LEDGER		ADJUSTMENTS		FINAL BALANCE	
	DEBIT	CREDIT	DEBIT	CREDIT	DEBIT	CREDIT
TOTALS						

- Long-term liabilities include all debts due beyond the next twelve months, and any deferred income.

Net Worth

- Net worth is the difference between assets and liabilities, consisting of capital stock, paid-in capital, retained earnings, and current net profits.

The balance sheet reports one line for each account within these groups. A summarized form of the major balance sheet groupings is shown in Figure B-4.

The income statement reports sales, direct costs, and expenses for a specified period of time. In most companies, the report drawn at the end of any month will show the year-to-date totals, compared to the identical period the year before.

The income statement includes these groupings:

Sales

- Gross revenue, less any returns and allowances.

Direct costs

- All costs directly related to the production of income, including materials purchased, direct labor, and other direct costs. Inventory levels are adjusted in this section as well.

Gross profit

- Sales minus direct costs.

General expenses

- The detailed income statement includes one line for each type of expense, either on the statement or by way of an attached schedule. Accounts with relatively small balances may be combined and reported as miscellaneous expenses. Expenses can also be subdivided as selling or variable expenses, and fixed or general and administrative expenses.

Figure B-4.
Balance sheet.

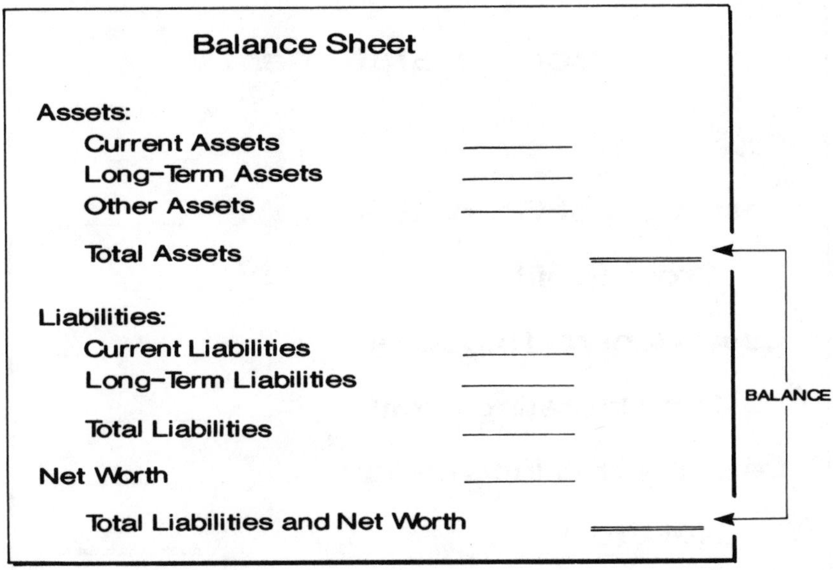

Balance Sheet

Assets:
- Current Assets ———————
- Long–Term Assets ———————
- Other Assets ———————

Total Assets ═══════

Liabilities:
- Current Liabilities ———————
- Long–Term Liabilities ———————

Total Liabilities ———————

Net Worth ———————

Total Liabilities and Net Worth ═══════

BALANCE

Net operating profit

- Gross profit minus expenses.

Federal income tax

- A provision for the tax liability.

Net profit

- Net operating (or pretax) profit, minus federal income tax.

Many companies will precede the last two sections with additional groupings for "other income" and "other expenses." These contain any nonoperational transactions, such as capital gains, interest income or expense, and foreign exchange rate changes. A summarized form of the income statement is shown in Figure B-5.

The statement of cash flows reports how cash was generated and used from operations, investments, and for pay-

Figure B-5.
Income statement.

```
┌─────────────────────────────────────────────────┐
│              Income Statement                   │
│                                                 │
│   Sales                            _____    │
│                                                 │
│   Less: Cost of Goods Sold         _____    │
│                                                 │
│       Gross Profit                 _____    │
│                                                 │
│   Less: General Expenses           _____    │
│                                                 │
│       Net Operating Profit         _____    │
│                                                 │
│   Less: Federal Income Tax         _____    │
│                                                 │
│       Net Profit                   =========    │
└─────────────────────────────────────────────────┘
```

ment of expenses, costs, and taxes. There are direct and indirect formats. Direct format reports greater detail and division of cash and will be used here. Sections include:

- Cash collected from customers
- Cash paid for inventory, for direct costs, or operating expenses
- Cash paid for income taxes

Categories requiring a breakdown beyond these general groups are shown below the summarized statement, as subschedules. Figure B-6 shows a summarized format for the statement of cash flows.

FOOTNOTES AND SCHEDULES

In addition to presenting the statements, some accounts require additional explanations. Footnotes explain relevant financial information not shown on the statements or expand on a reported number. Examples include:

- Explanation of inventory valuation method
- Commitments not reported as liabilities, such as long-term leases
- Contingent liabilities, such as judgments that might be decided against the company for pending lawsuits
- Extraordinary items, including large write-offs of obsolete inventory or bad debts, or a one-time profit or loss from changes in exchange rates
- Explanation of the method used to compute a reserve for bad debts
- The current market value of real estate, compared to reported cost-less-depreciation value on the balance sheet

Figure B-6.
Statement of cash flows.

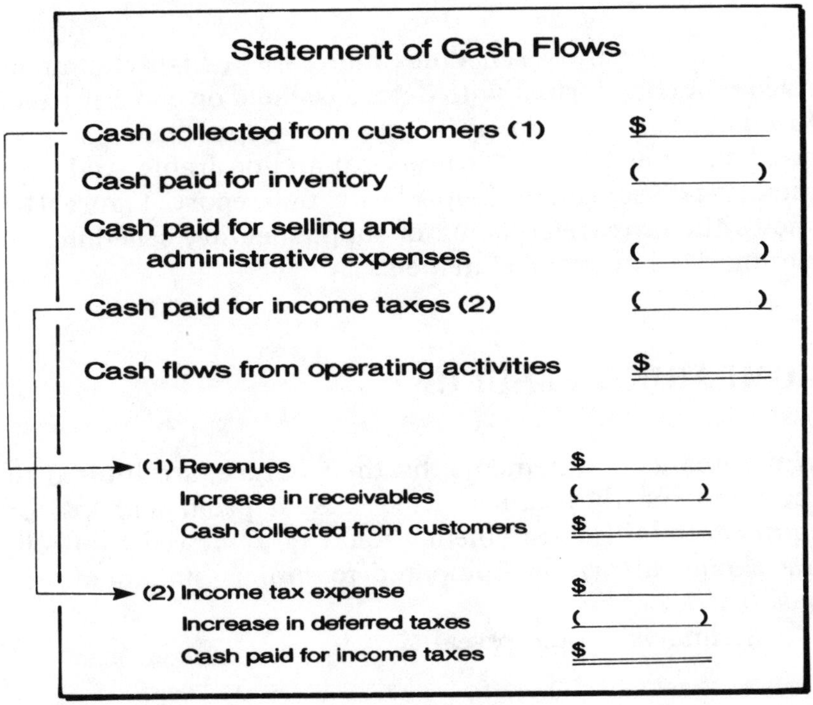

Any number of additional footnotes might be included with financial statements. Information in the footnotes can be more important than what's reported on the statements themselves. The additional information fills a gap that would otherwise make financial statements inaccurate and, in some cases, misleading.

In addition to footnotes, a financial statement may be shown in highly summarized form, with certain classifications or groups broken down on supplementary schedules or exhibits, including

- A breakdown of the net worth section, with beginning balances, changes, and ending balances for each component (capital stock, paid-in capital, retained earnings)
- Detail listing of general expenses, when a one-line total is reported on the income statement
- A listing of long-term assets, showing the basis, depreciation, and net value

Supplementary schedules allow for a highly summarized reporting format with details isolated on another page. In companies with many accounts to report, the summarized statement format is practical and desirable, and supplementary schedules help clarify the report. Figure B-7 shows the cross-referencing of supplementary schedules to summarized financial statements.

COMPARING RESULTS

While financial statements, by their nature, are limited to the numbers, they can be used to spot profit and loss or equity trends. No statement should be reviewed by itself, but should always be compared to similar statements for past periods.

An analysis could reveal:

Figure B-7.
Supplementary schedule.

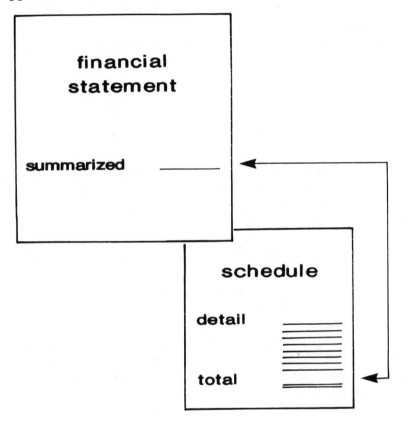

- A trend toward increasing long-term debt, meaning capitalization is shifting away from investors and more toward lenders; also meaning that debt service is rising and placing greater demands on cash flow
- A steady rise in sales volume combined with a consistent ratio of gross and net profits
- A consistent level of fixed expenses when sales are on the rise
- Growth in the average balance of outstanding accounts receivable, exceeding the rate of growth in sales volume

Each trend reveals something significant to management. If a trend is negative, action must be taken to reverse the trend; if positive, it means that management is doing its job correctly.

Financial statements are usually prepared in comparative form, in one of three ways:

1. By amount. The current figures are compared to the same results from the previous year. This comparative method is the most popular.

2. By percentage of change. This format, most applicable to a detailed listing of expenses, is popular for internal-use-only statements, showing the percentage increase or decrease from the previous year.

Another percentage format is to assume that sales represent 100 percent, and each cost or expense and profits are reported as a portion of sales. This familiar report loses accuracy if sales levels change drastically from one year to the next.

3. Combined form. Both the amount and percentage change are shown, enabling management to review either or both, which helps spot trends and relevant changes in net worth and profits.

Figure B-8 summarizes the three types of comparative reports.

Financial statements do not reveal everything important in the organization. The restrictive accounting rules prevent current market valuation from being included, a rule aimed at preventing abuse and equalizing reporting standards. And the liability of a long-term lease commitment or pending lawsuit judgments, while potentially substantial, are reported only by footnote.

An additional problem arises when management judges a company solely on the basis of the numbers. The quality of

Figure B-8.
Comparative statements.

by amount

DESCRIPTION	AMOUNT	
	THIS YEAR	LAST YEAR

by percentage

DESCRIPTION	AMOUNT		%
	THIS YEAR	LAST YEAR	CHANGE

combined form

DESCRIPTION	THIS YEAR		LAST YEAR		CHANGE	
	AMOUNT	%	AMOUNT	%	AMOUNT	%

management, labor relations, internal morale, human relations philosophy and practice, and a number of other intangible factors all determine a company's financial health. A dollar value cannot be placed on intangible factors; so fair and complete analysis must include nonfinancial realities in addition to financial statements.

Glossary

accrual accounting A method of reporting financial results calling for adjustments to reflect income in the period earned (but not necessarily collected), and costs and expenses in the period incurred (but not necessarily paid). Accrual accounting is more accurate than cash accounting as it reports results consistently and reflects true activity rather than transaction dates.

accrual journal A journal entry prepared to place an accrued value into the books and records.

accumulated value of 1 A compound interest calculation to estimate the future value of a single deposit, assuming compounding of a specified interest rate for a specified period of time.

accumulated value of 1 per period A compound interest calculation to estimate the future value of a series of deposits, assuming compounding of a specified interest rate for a specified period of time.

after-tax profit The amount of profit earned by a company after deducting an allowance for federal income tax liabilities.

allocation The assignment of costs and expenses to several departments, based on an assumed split such as number of employees, floor space, or usage.

amortization payments A compound interest calculation to estimate the amount of period payments that must be made to retire a debt, assuming compounding of a specified interest rate for a specified period of time.

annual compounding A method of computing compound interest in which a previous year's deposit is increased by the nominal, or stated, rate of interest.

annualized yield The percentage earned or paid, expressed on a twelve-month basis. When a yield applies to a period shorter or longer than one year, it is annualized to reflect consistent and comparative periods.

assets The properties owned by a company; in comparison, liabilities are the company's debts.

assumption base The information used to justify a budgeted level of income, costs, expenses, or cash flow, used to compare to actual results and identify causes of variances.

audit trail The process employed by accountants and auditors to verify transactions and to trace a final value back through the books to a series of source documents or to prove a computation by tracing the conclusion back to source information.

balance sheet A financial statement that summarizes a company's assets, liabilities, and net worth as of a specified date.

bar graph A graph involving one or more values represented on a scale, reported as of a single moment or for comparative periods.

books of final entry The general ledger, where all detailed transactions are summarized in preparation for financial statements. Details supporting the entries are found in the books of original entry (journals), and source documents (vouchers, receipts, etc.).

books of original entry The journals, where all detailed transactions are recorded. The summarized total of these entries is later posted to the ledger, also called the books of final entry.

budget An estimate or standard of future costs and expenses, intended as a means for testing controls and reaching financial goals.

budgeting process A term describing the process of estimating the future, divided into three groups: income forecasts, cost and expense budgets, and cash flow projections.

business plan A strategic document and process, including evaluation of competition and the market; supply and demand; forecasts, budgets, and projections; and stated goals for a specified period of time.

capital expenditure The investment of funds in an asset that will be useful for a number of years as opposed to current costs and expenses required to operate the business. A capital expenditure must be depreciated over a period of time.

capitalization The collective funds used to organize and operate a business. It consists of two primary groups: equity capital (stockholders' equity, paid-in capital, and retained earnings) and debt capital (loans, bonds, and other amounts owed).

cash accounting An accounting method in which entries go into the books only when cash changes hands. While more simple than accrual accounting, this method is also less accurate. Earned income and incurred costs and expenses will be reported only when cash changes hands.

centralized budget A budgeting process in which the responsibility, reporting, and response are controlled in one department.

circle graph A graph showing the division of an assumed whole, into parts, with percentages reflected as degrees of the full circle.

collection ratio A ratio that estimates the average number of days required to collect outstanding accounts receivable, useful in following trends. The average accounts receivable balance is divided by the average daily charge sales to arrive at the number of days.

compound interest A method for accumulating interest in which accumulated past interest, plus principal, earns a greater amount of interest in the subsequent period.

cost center A department, section, or division identified for the purpose of allocating or budgeting.

cost of goods sold The total amount of direct costs, adjusted for changes in inventory level. When deducted from sales for a period of time, the net result is a company's gross profit.

credit The right side of an entry in the double-entry bookkeeping system.

current assets Cash or assets convertible to cash within the next twelve months, including accounts receivable, marketable securities, current notes receivable, and inventory.

current liabilities Debts that are payable within the next twelve months, including twelve payments on long-term notes, and current operating accruals, taxes, and other liabilities.

current ratio A ratio comparing current assets to current liabilities, to judge the relative health of a company's cash flow.

current yield The percentage of yield being earned based on current value of the investment adjusted for premium or discount.

daily compounding A method of compound interest in which the annual rate is divided by 360 (or 365), and the previous day's balance is increased by the daily rate.

debit The left side of an entry in the double-entry bookkeeping system.

debt capital Funds raised by incurring debt, through notes, bonds, and other liabilities.

decentralized budget A budgeting process in which each department, section, or division is responsible for developing, reporting, and controlling its own budget.

depreciation A noncash expense to record a partial recognition of the cost of capital assets.

direct costs Expenditures directly related to the generation of income, which will vary according to the volume of revenue.

disbursements journal A journal used to record and classify payments.

double-entry system The procedure used for recording and controlling financial transactions. Each entry contains two equal sides, a debit and a credit. When books are posted correctly, the two sides will always balance.

equity capital That portion of total capitalization belonging to ownership interests of stockholders.

favorable variance A condition resulting when actual income is greater than forecast or when costs or expenses are lower than budgeted allowances.

financial statement A report prepared to reveal a company's assets, liabilities, and net worth (balance sheet); profit or loss from operations (income statement); or the use of cash (statement of cash flows).

fixed expenses Also called overhead, those expenses that are not expected to vary significantly with changes in sales volume.

forecast An estimate of future revenues, used to set standards, monitor progress, and establish controls for a specified period of time.

future value The value of money at a time in the future, given an assumption about a rate of interest and method of compounding.

general journal A specialized journal used to prepare entries not appropriate for the cash receipts or for the cash disbursements journal. These include noncash expenses, accruals and reversals, and adjustments.

general ledger The permanent summarized record of all company transactions used to prepare financial statements and reflecting the permanent record of entries.

gross profit   The amount a company earns, after revenues are reduced by direct costs (purchases, direct labor, and changes in inventory level).

horizontal bar graph   A bar graph in which value is reflected from top to bottom, with stationary distribution reflected from left to right.

income statement   A financial statement that reports a company's sales, direct costs, expenses, and profit for a period of time.

intangible assets   Assets carried on the books that do not have physical value. These include assigned value of goodwill and covenants not to compete, for example.

interpolation   An estimate of a value, based on known values above and below the one desired. This technique is used for estimating compound interest factors for rates of interest in between those listed on tables.

inventory turnover   A ratio used to judge efficiency in average inventory levels. The cost of goods sold is divided by the average inventory level to determine the number of times, on average, the full inventory was replaced during the year.

journal   A book used to record a transaction from a source document, check, or receipt. Specialized transactions are recorded in their own journal (receipts, disbursements, and general), and summarized totals are transferred to the general ledger.

ledger   A book used to record summarized transactions from journals, to prepare financial statements, and to accumulate a permanent record of company activity.

liabilities   The company's debts; in comparison, assets are the properties owned by the company.

line graph   A graph representing changes in value over time, in a visual rather than numerical way, using solid or broken lines on a scale.

long-term assets   Assets with value beyond the current year, which are capitalized and written off by way of depreciation.

long-term liabilities   Debts of the company that are due within the coming twelve months.

monthly compounding A method of computing compound interest in which the annual rate is divided by 12, and applied to each previous month's accumulated balance.

net profit The amount of money earned for a period of time after reducing sales by direct costs, expenses, and liability for federal income taxes.

net worth The capital of a company, representing the difference between assets and liabilities and consisting of shareholders' equity (in a corporation), paid-in capital, and retained earnings.

nominal rate A stated annual interest rate, without adjustment for current yield based on premium or discount of the principal amount, and without consideration of compounding method.

operating profit The profit earned by a company, represented by sales minus operating costs and expenses, but before allowing for interest income or expense, other nonoperational adjustments, and federal income tax liabilities.

overhead Expenses of the company that are fixed or permanent and will not vary with the level of sales.

pie chart Alternative name for the circle graph.

present value of 1 A compound interest calculation to estimate the amount of a single deposit required today to reach a target amount in the future, assuming compounding of a specified interest rate for a specified period of time.

present value of 1 per period A compound interest calculation to estimate the amount of a series of deposits required to fund a future series of payments, assuming compounding of a specified interest rate for a specified period of time.

pretax profit The amount of net profit with operating net adjusted for nonoperational income and expense but before federal income tax liabilities are deducted.

profit and loss statement An alternative name for the income statement.

profit center An identified division, section, or department responsible for generating and controlling profits.

projection An estimate of future cash flow changes, intended as a monitoring procedure to anticipate cash availability and plan accordingly.

quarterly compounding A method of computing compound interest in which the annual rate is divided by four and the resulting interest rate applied to the previous quarter's accumulated balance.

quick assets ratio A ratio comparing current assets, without inventory, to current liabilities.

ratio A summarized comparison between two related values, reflected as a percentage, fraction, or the number of times an event occurs. The ratio is used as a tool for financial reporting.

receipts journal A journal designed to record income or payments received against outstanding accounts receivable. Summarized totals are posted to the general ledger each month.

reconciliation The identification and verification of an account's contents, including entry of all needed adjustments.

return on equity The net profits for a year divided by the value of shareholders' equity at the beginning of the year.

return on sales The net profits for a year divided by the amount of sales.

semiannual compounding A method of computing compound interest in which the annual rate of interest is divided by two and the resulting half-year rate applied to the previous balance.

significant variance A variance that must be explained, as defined by standards of a company's budgeting procedure. Significance is defined as a combination of variance percentage and amount.

simple interest A method for paying interest in which no accumulated interest is subject to subsequent interest payments. The interest paid is based only on the principal amount.

sinking fund factors A compound interest calculation to estimate the amount of a series of deposits required to reach a target amount in the future, assuming compounding of a specified interest rate for a specified period of time.

source document A receipt, voucher, or invoice that proves the validity and nature of a business transaction.

statement of cash flows A financial statement that shows how cash balances changed during the year, identifying sources of money as well as spendings and the net amount of change.

subsidiary account A specialized subsection of the accounting records, designed to manage a large amount of transactions of one type. The total changes for the month are reported in the general ledger.

T-account   The summary of entries in an account, used to analyze and reconcile activity or to summarize a range of related transactions.

tangible net worth   The net worth of a company, reduced for the reported value of intangible assets.

trend analysis   The study of values and related values expressed through ratios for the purpose of identifying emerging trends and actions required to reverse negatives.

turnover in working capital   A ratio comparing sales and working capital (the difference between current assets and current liabilities). Sales for a specified period of time are divided by the working capital net amount.

unfavorable variance   A variance involving actual costs or expenses greater than year-to-date budgeted amounts or revenue below year-to-date forecast.

variable expenses   Expenses that will vary, to a degree, based on changes in sales volume and activity but that are not directly related to sales as are direct costs.

variance   The difference between an expected total (budget) and the actual total in an account.

vertical bar graph   A bar graph in which value is reported from left to right and a stationary distribution is shown from top to bottom.

working capital   The difference between current assets and current liabilities, available to the company to fund operations.

Index